THE TABLE AT THE END OF THE WORLD

THE TABLE AT THE END OF THE WORLD

Christ's Regard for Those in Despair

John Andrew Bryant

BakerBooks
a division of Baker Publishing Group
Grand Rapids, Michigan

Published by Baker Books
a division of Baker Publishing Group
Grand Rapids, Michigan
BakerBooks.com

Printed in the United States of America

ISBN 9781540906151 (paper)
ISBN 9781493465453 (ebook)

Editorial by Todd Hains, Ethan McCarthy, Jessi Strong, Mandi Newell
Cover design by Laura Klynstra
Interior design by Abigail Stocker

Baker Publishing Group publications use paper produced from sustainable forestry practices and postconsumer waste whenever possible.

26 27 28 29 30 31 32 7 6 5 4 3 2 1

To my father, who taught me how to be gentle
and how to make a place of rest by saying,
"How 'bout a cake and a Coke?"

CONTENTS

For what we proclaim is not ourselves, but Jesus Christ as Lord,
with ourselves as your servants for Jesus' sake. For God,
who said, "Let light shine out of darkness," has shone
in our hearts to give the light of the knowledge
of the glory of God in the face of Jesus Christ.

—2 Corinthians 4:5–6

Lighten our darkness, we beseech you, O Lord,
and by your great mercy defend us from
all perils and dangers of this night,
for the love of your only Son,
our Savior, Jesus Christ.
Amen.

1

THE FEAST OF BREAD AND LIGHT

*Another word for Christ Himself—
He says He is the Bread of Life and
Light of the World, and we are told
in Scripture to keep the feast*

I'M SITTING WITH OLD MEN ON A STOOP while they smoke the world's cheapest cigarettes. The kind with flavors like blueberry, vanilla, and "smooth," where the stuff spills out of the bottom of the cigarette when they take the cigarette out. They love them and I think it's funny they love them, and I almost don't mind the smoke coming my way.

I'm not that old and I don't smoke but I'm with all the old men who do. I'm with all the crusty locals. Dark sunburnt skin, dusty caps, canes and electric chairs. I'm here and I'm not even from here. But we're talking. It's been years of sitting here, and we're finally talking.

WE'RE TALKING ABOUT HOW OLD EVERYONE IS and how old everyone looks. About who's coming by and who's going to stay inside. And what they're serving at the soup kitchen. And what they found crawling in their bed last night. And what kind of boots rip off your toenails if you walk in them too long. And whether spring's coming or not coming.

These things we have to talk about. This small talk. This place we meet. This way to be together.

We have to have small talk. We have to share in something to see each other clearly. And if we do not share in something, we cannot see each other clearly. And I want to see them clearly.

I take the word *share* literally. One of the men regularly offers me a Zebra Cake, and once—right before I was preaching—a piece of cooked Spam. I take it from his crusty cigarette hands and put it in my mouth so that we've shared in something and seen each other clearly.

But most of the time it isn't Spam, or Zebra Cakes. It's just this stoop. We share this stoop and all the time we've wasted on this stoop.

The stoop marks the furthest edge of our downtown church. It sits at the edge of a four-way stop, and from it you can see the world come and go. It feels like the furthest outpost of our church. The old men sit here, and I sit here with them.

They come out here when it's hard to be in church. When it all gets to be too much. It's easier for them to be out here. It's easier for me to be out here too.

Their eyes flash warmth—a recognition and delight. This is our time together. They know how to hang and shoot the breeze and be with people. And I'm learning that too. I'm learning how to be here, how to just visit. This stoop, this time, a thing shared between us. There is an ease, a rapport. And I know this is the place I'm supposed to be.

I try to always take the Zebra Cakes and the pieces of cooked Spam from their fingers. Every now and then they'll even offer me one of those nasty old cigarettes that spill out the bottom and

I'll take it too as a keepsake. I keep a stack of them in my office as a sign of mutual honor and respect.

These old men, at the furthest edge of our downtown church. All our crusty locals. The place where they smoke and the place where I gel pen. The place where everyone else walks on by.

It's real cold and the cigarettes burn real slow. When it's cold it's really cold out here on this stoop, and when it's hot it's really hot out here on this stoop.

Right now it's really cold, and I don't know if I can stand to sit much longer and hold these gel pens in my cold, cold hands. But it's been years of baking and shivering out here, years of just visiting. And we're finally talking. It's cold out here but they want to tell me things now. Toenails, bedbugs, the weather, and the food at the soup kitchen. But also the loved ones who've died, the messed-up things they've seen. The things they just don't understand.

I think of the strange banquet all this small talk is. This small talk, this regard, all this wasted time.

All because I came out here and waited for what they wanted to say and whether they wanted to say it. I think that means I'm staying.

I know they like me because they like to make fun of me, and I'm allowed to make fun of them. They often ask me if I'm going outside to color with my gel pens and if I say I am they'll often come out there with me to smoke. And all of a sudden there we are. At this strange feast.

They say, "You coloring?"

They smirk and smile. And I'm being made fun of. But it probably doesn't matter.

I say, "I'll color, you smoke, we'll call it even."

The gel pens help me concentrate on the good news coming to me through the promises of Scripture. I'm on the stoop with a few old men, underlining the promises of Scripture with a big ol' bag of gel pens. This strange life I have in Christ. How I take hold of Him and how He takes hold of me. How I hear His news and sit at His feast. Whatever it takes to do just that. Whatever it takes, even if it's gel pens. The slow pondering of this good news, the gel pens in my cold, cold hands. Sitting at the feast while they blow all that friendly, sweet-smelling, nasty ol' smoke in my face.

Hearing this good news: that Jesus Christ is Lord and Savior. That Christ has died, Christ is risen, and Christ will come again. That the forgiveness of sins and the gift of the Holy Spirit is now offered in His name. This good news isn't just information. It is the light that reveals Him, the bread by which He gives Himself to us.

This good news: who He is, what He's done, and what it means for us.

We need this good news. A Christian is someone who hears this news and receives this mercy. The sweet mercy of Christ Himself.

That good news coming to us through the words of Scripture. Words I underline with a big ol' bag of gel pens.

A man on this stoop once said, "There's nothing left to do, Jesus already did it." And I suppose that's right. Jesus has already done it. There is only this feast. The feast is who He is and what He's done. What do you do when there's nothing left but to share in who He is and what He's done? When there is nothing left but who we are at this table? Nothing but the offer of bread and the shining of light? Nothing left but to go do this and share in Christ together?

If there's something I know, it's that I can sit at this table and share in this feast by just being here. We offer bread and shine that light by just being here.

Trading stories, trading small talk and regard. The gentleness close at hand. The joy we offer, the joy in offering. Sharing in something and seeing each other clearly. The one we share in when we share in something like this. A life in Christ that includes me seeing them, them seeing me.

WHY AM I OUT HERE on the stoop like this, in the furnace of all this wasted time?

The closest parallel I've found is a trip to Grandma's house. The existential adventure of a trip to Grandma's house.

Everyone knows there's nothing to do at Grandma's house. Sometimes you fix things at Grandma's house, or bring her something. But everyone knows the only reason you go to Grandma's house is to see Grandma.

Sometimes it's Reese's Cups instead of Zebra Cakes. Or banana pudding instead of Spam. Or cinnamon disks and

Werther's Originals instead of cheap cigarettes. Or a porch swing instead of a stoop.

But the point is the same: to visit, to trade stories and regard, to make small talk, to share in something, and to see each other clearly. A life in Christ that includes them seeing me, me seeing them.

I remember at some point I would just sprawl out on the floor and sink into all the plush carpet of Grandma's house, accepting the fact that there's nothing to do at Grandma's house but just be at Grandma's house. You arrive at just being there. You sink down in the plush carpet and partake of the incarnate funk of just being here. Sinking down into the furnace of all that wasted time. That is when you've become pure gift, pure presence. Saying what you say by just being here: that you love Grandma and that she's worth going to see.

That is what I mean by just sitting here on this stoop. Finally learning to just sit here: the story of the last five years. The last five years have been one long sad beautiful trip to Grandma's house. Except her house is a stoop or a bench or a porch or a dirty hospital room. Except that Grandma has been crushed by what life's like, and Grandma is anxious, sad, and possibly dangerous.

I'm in awe of the men on this stoop. All the old, sad, crispy men out here in the sun. All my sad Grandmas. I'm in awe of all they've lost and all the trouble they're in and all the lies they've been told. How they've made a life in this place where the worst happens and nothing makes sense and everything falls apart. The glory of their sad, tired faces.

I'm in awe of this realization: that there's something worse than all you've lost and all the trouble you're in and all the lies you've been told, and it's when it doesn't matter to you or anyone else. That would be the worst thing: to be all alone with all you've lost and all the trouble you're in and all the lies you've been told, out here where the worst happens and nothing makes sense and everything falls apart. What's life if there's no one to share the worst of it with? To share in Christ together, even if it's awful.

I often think about how a lot of ministry is simply making sure the worst doesn't happen. That kids turn out alright, that young families turn out alright, that college kids turn out alright. But with a lot of the folks I'm with, the damage has been done. The worst has already happened. They've already lost everything. I think of how a lot of ministry is designed to help people get better. But is that what ministry is about? Making sure people get better? What happens when they can't, or won't? Are people still worth seeing even if they won't get better?

If there's something I'm afraid of, it's what happens when Christians are no longer known for visiting the people the worst has happened to. When we decide ministry is for making people better instead of announcing this Person—announcing that nothing that happens can change what life's about. That we still minister, even when and especially when people won't get better. We go and visit the people whose world has ended, and we set up a table at the end of the world.

And so I'm out here on this stoop. Out here where things don't get better. Out here where you have to know how to hang.

Out here where small talk is essential. The gentle song and dance of a good visit. The back and forth and sway of it. Not to help them or give advice or tell them what to do. Not while they've got their cheap cigarettes and I've got my gel pens and we're all talking about toenails and the weather. You can't sit here and do that to people. But you can hold gel pens in your cold, cold hands. You can say the thing you say by just being here.

It's not a place you give advice, but it is a place you make announcements. That it's cold, or hot. That the soup kitchen food was good today. That certain boots rip your toenails off. That someone's sick, that someone's doing better.

I am here to make an announcement. Just visiting makes the announcement: that they're worth being around. That I want to be around them. That if it's a waste of time, then they're worth wasting time on.

Visiting is its own song about a feast. Its own word about that Word. It is the vindication of good news, its own sign that this news is true.

I'm here making an announcement. That it's cold. That I've got gel pens and they've got cigarettes. That the soup kitchen food was good. That someone's doing better. That spring isn't here yet. That they're worth being around.

And that Christ has died, Christ is risen, and Christ will come again.

I'm a sign, I hope, of this: that they are on a long journey out of pride and lies through trouble and loss toward meaning and rest. That Christ is the way out of pride and lies, the way through trouble and loss, and that He is the meaning and rest they're headed toward. That Christ is their companion, and I am just a sign of His company. Just being here: our quiet sign of the Person this is all about. So that every visit is an announcement of the gospel. Our announcement that this news is true.

Before it's a special feeling or a relationship, the gospel is an announcement of something that's true, the report of an event in history. The announcement of who Christ is and what Christ has done and what it means for us.

I'm not that into having nasty smoke in my face, or just sitting on a stoop and burning in the sun or blistering in the cold.

I like these guys, but I'm not here because I like them. Liking them is not a good enough reason to be out here. I'm here because Christ has died, Christ is risen, and Christ will come again. I'm here because this news is true. I'm here because Ordinary Hospitality is our sign that this news is true.

I'm here because just being here announces that, makes it clear. Or at least, clearer than it was before.

Don't get me wrong—I really do enjoy them. But there are days when I don't, and I'm still here.

Other people are never a good enough reason to do something, but the Lord's mercy always is. This bread and this light are themselves a good enough reason to offer them. This is my announcement. The mercy we announce by just being here.

No matter how wild and ruthless and beautiful their talk, that is what I mean by being here. That is what I announce: His mercy, His news, His feast. This sign that this news is true: Christ has died, Christ is risen, Christ will come again. That is why we visit people who won't get better. To remind them, and to remind ourselves.

I BELIEVE THAT VISITING PEOPLE is the offer of bread and the shining of light—our most basic, tender, and visible sign of the reality of Christ, the forgiveness of sins, and the homecoming offered only in Him. It is the song by which Christ gathers a people to Himself. Our song about His feast.

If there's something I'm worried about, it's that we have lost our most basic, tender, and visible sign of Him. That we are no longer known for visiting the people the worst has happened to. That in our rush to make disciples and defend our faith we have lost this quiet sign of Christ. We've lost the thing we say by just being here.

I often look into the mirror and find the eyes of a crusty local looking back at me. My mannerisms slower, my lumbering body draped in a droopier flannel, my glasses crooked and scratched, my eyes a little more wrinkly, my skin a little more leathery. A little wall-eyed. A little worse for wear. My own sad Grandma.

And who am I? A would-be pastor, now a part-time chaplain. Just a big ol' man in flannel with a big ol' bag of gel pens with a bunch of crusty locals. Just sitting here with gel pens and good news. Here to say what we say by just sitting here.

It's taken years, but I can finally say there's nowhere else I'd rather be. Out here with them. Because there's nothing left but to share in who He is and what He's done by just being here. Nothing left but who we are at this table. Nothing but the offer of bread and the shining of light. Nothing to do but get crispy and crusty on this stoop, at this feast.

The joy we offer; the joy in offering. The one we share in whenever we share something, even if it's just this small talk, this visit, this way to be together, this place we meet. The Person this is all about.

OUT HERE IS WHERE I'm supposed to be. Out here I run the risk of feeling like myself again. And it has taken a long time to start feeling that way, after I crashed and burned on the idea of myself as a pastor.

Even if there's no one there, it feels like a place of rest to me. All my life has felt like a search for this rest—and the only rest I've found is at this feast. To go do this and share in Christ together. Out here exposed to everything, out here where the worst happens and nothing makes sense and everything falls apart.

That is the only rest I've found: hearing good news and being out here. Cleansed and presented by this good news. Presented as this offering, all through His Spirit and all of it a mending.

Out here the bleak gray parts of life take on a darker shade of blue. Blue is the color of my life, the color I want my life to be. A color that's quiet, simple, gentle. The color of stillness, patience, sorrow, waiting, and longing. It is an Advent color, a color that gets brighter when it gets darker.

Out here, the bleak gray parts of life take on brighter light and a darker shade of blue, and the bleak gray parts of life begin to take on a stench, the blessed stench of beauty, goodness, and truth. There is a stench to just being here. The incarnate funk of just being here.

And all of it, this color, this light, this stench, has a smudge to it: this life blurring to the world to come. When the Lord comes back, we'll serve Him in His temple, which is heaven and earth. God has given us gifts, and we'll offer then what we can offer now: our service, our gifts. Ministry is about offering now what we'll offer then. Offering those things now, serving that temple now. When we do, there is a holy smudge to things—the smudge of glory: this life blurring with the world to come.

I'm speaking of that darker shade of blue, that brighter light, that blessed stench, that incarnate funk, and that smudge of glory all at once when I say that hearing good news and being out here is the only kind of life that ever struck that deeper note of rest. Good news and Ordinary Hospitality—the only kind of life that has ever struck that deeper note of rest.

Rest is what we offer. Rest is what makes me feel like myself again. Its light is bright. Its color blue. Its stench blessed, its smudge holy. Rest is gel pens and cheap cigarettes. Rest is hearing good news and just being out here. To go do this and share in Christ together.

Another word for rest is *joy*. Joy and gladness. A gladness that is clear and bright and sad as well. A clear bright joyful longing sadness. The deep, solemn gladness of a wounded, lovely, selfish person given to wounded, lovely, selfish people. The signs of Christ Himself. A Christ who gives us back to God, ourselves, and each other.

IT WAS A LONG TIME before I even sat on stoops. It was only after my career as a pastor got good and ruined, only after I'd been crushed by what life is like. Only after I crashed and burned on an idea of myself.

I would only start sitting on stoops five years after that. Five years I spent learning how to be a part-time chaplain instead of a full-time pastor. The five years I spent learning how to be with people again, learning how to be given back to others. A long, slow, five-year walk out of pride and lies, through trouble and loss, toward meaning and rest. A long, slow walk I took with Christ. A long, slow walk with His Spirit. A long, slow walk toward this stoop.

It was only on a barefoot late-night summer walk, as I finished this book, that I realized that those five years had become a memory, a place I was finally out of and could now look back on.

Those five years felt like their own wild country, a separate geography in the rearview mirror of my life: a blessed and bitter time, a special time of anguish and light. Those five years were a strange land that held all my longing and sorrow.

Time spent learning how to be with people again. To be with wounded, lovely, selfish people again after wounded, lovely, selfish people had destroyed me.

It is my job to be with people now. My ministry is the long, slow walk we take together. Christ is their companion and I am only the sign of His company. My job is hearing good news and just being out here, out here as a sign that this news is true. I've finally arrived at just sitting here.

But only after I made my way across that wild country, that special time of anguish and light. That wild country where I learned my job was to just be with people who weren't doing well. My primary job wasn't preaching or teaching, but Ordinary Hospitality, the gift of regard, the gentleness close at hand.

The Lord showed me how to be with people again when for so long other people were a bitter feast. The Lord showed me how to sit at the bitter feast of others and to know that the bitter feast is Christ as well. Somehow Christ is there as well. The one who's there whenever wounded, lovely, selfish people are given to wounded, lovely, selfish people.

And I can honestly say I mostly enjoy people now. I especially enjoy my stoop friends. I believe this enjoyment—this recognition and delight—is the radiance of Christ. I have a lot of anxiety and a bit of depression, and this recognition and delight always feels like a revelation to me and perhaps to them. How deep and bright and sad it is when I find it, when I feel it again. I'm still shaken by the clear bright joy of it. That deep gladness. This sudden rapport and delight. The smudge of glory, the blessed stench. The color blue. The clear sound of that deeper note of rest. Hearing good news and just being out here, sharing in Christ together.

It is my joy and honor and calling to be with them, to be here on the stoop and to give regard to baffling old men. The gel pens and the cheap cigarettes. The blessed stench of our time together.

I watch them smoke the world's cheapest cigarettes down to nubs and see how far they flick them. I'm here for how far they flick them. Its long arc, my laughter at how far it'll go when they flick. My favorite place, my favorite people.

And for it to all be called joy.

This recognition and delight. Here for all of it. All their ruthless tender heartless wild wonderful talk. The word for wasted time is joy.

These men, these old men—my sorrow and my joy. All they've lost, all the lies they've been told, all the trouble they're in. All the things that have happened.

The cheap cigarettes and the broken-down wheelchairs. The things they say so shocking and baffling and awful, the life they've had to live so shocking and baffling and awful. And not, it seems, like mine at all. And yet they are lovely. They're lovely to me. They've seen too much, gone through too much. Seen and done too many terrible things. And I all I want to do is to visit them. And be there with them and see the glory of their sad, tired faces.

I long for them to be okay and for them to have a place of rest. A sign of rest in this place where the worst happens and nothing makes sense and everything falls apart.

I know we're different, but I know that is what we all want. I've never met anyone who didn't just want to be okay, who didn't want a place of rest. And I long for them to have something like that. When all of life is so messed up, in this place of pride and lies, trouble and loss, chaos and disaster.

Everyone I know is on a long sad journey out of pride and lies, through trouble and loss, toward that meaning and rest. A journey they make with Christ. A journey they make with Christ as their companion and me a sign of His company.

Out here where every visit is a darker shade of blue. Where every visit must have that blessed stench. Sharing in who He is and what He's done by just being here.

I've driven all night before, just to make it to this stoop, just to be with them, just in case I'd see someone I needed to see, just in case they'd say what they'd need to say. That's what so much of this wasted time is: waiting for people to say what they need to say, and only if they want to say it.

I've driven all night just to be out here, because that is what seems worth doing. This is where I end up when I hear good news, where good news takes me, and where my life seems to be. I've driven all night because there's nothing left but to share in who He is and what He's done.

The only rest I've found: hearing good news and just being out here. Cleansed and presented by this good news. Presented on this stoop, and all through His Spirit and all of it a mending.

I've found rest here, and rest—for me—is when there's finally something life's about. Rest is the joy of finding there's still a Person this is all about.

It's always a surprise for me to find out there is still a Person this is all about, given what life is often like, given all we've lost, all the trouble we're in, and all the lies we've been told. Given that we are subject to forces that are completely beyond us and beyond any of the words we have. Forces that take away words, so that we have no words for everything coming toward us and everything going on inside us.

Nothing is right; everything is all messed up. And yet I still believe there is a Person this is all about—and that is joy. He is joy. And joy is meaning and rest in this place where the worst happens and nothing makes sense and everything falls apart. Joy is solid ground in this place of pride and lies, trouble and loss, chaos and disaster.

Joy is the Person in this place. Joy is Christ Himself: the joy we offer and the joy in offering. The bread we eat, the light we see, the news we've heard, the mercy we receive. The feast itself. I believe in joy. I believe in the Feast of Bread and Light.

THIS JOY WILL ALWAYS HAVE a solemn hold on me. That light, that color, that stench, that deeper note of rest. Those strange signs of Christ Himself.

He is joy and His joy is to have His people back. To have the crusty locals back. To have the old men on this stoop back. The old men who've had to see so many shocking and baffling and awful things. The beautiful wild ruthless men. The baffled old men Christ has offered Himself to.

He is joy. And His joy is to have His people back. And our joy, our only real joy, is to be given in His name to His joy. To offer those things by which Christ gathers a people to Himself, to share in who He is and what He's done. To offer bread and hold out that light.

When I first started this work, another man on this stoop—a handsome, long-haired friend of mine with acute schizophrenia—looked at me.

"I got the Holy Spirit," he said. "I got the Holy Spirit, and now I don't know what to do."

I looked at him. I didn't know either. I was a would-be pastor who'd lost his career. Who'd been crushed: spiritually abused by a pastor, abandoned by my denomination, and deeply alienated from the evangelical movement. Who'd crashed and burned on an idea of himself.

I was still in ministry, but just barely. And only doing this. A would-be pastor, now a kinda sorta chaplain, with an organization that offered a listening presence to folks on the street, that called itself a ministry of presence. I was an orthodox Christian, I knew that. I had the Holy Spirit. And I didn't know what to do.

It took all those years, but the Holy Spirit finally got me to sit there on that stoop, to give regard, to waste all that time. And to call it joy.

I think I know now what the Holy Spirit wants: for us to share in who Christ is and what He's done. To eat bread and see light. To offer bread and hold out light. To cleanse us with this news and present us this offering.

After I'd been abused, abandoned, and alienated, the Holy Spirit was still doing that. That Holy Spirit there with me in that wild country of those bitter years, with me in that special time of anguish and light. To cleanse me with this news and present me as this offering, until a would-be pastor was finally just on this stoop. Given in His name. Given to His joy. Giving a more Ordinary Hospitality.

Out here learning about His joy. Out here learning the fierce song of gentleness, grief, and gladness.

Because that's what I think His joy is: the gentleness, grief, and gladness that is His cross. A cross that is His joy. Because His joy is to have his people back.

And being out on this stoop is my sign of the cross. I think again of when I was supposed to be a pastor: how I used to be very busy. I was told I was a gifted preacher, I was told I was supposed to do a church plant. I was told I was supposed to build something great. I had that career I was talking about. And what I do now is try to honor and uphold and welcome by just being here.

I WAS TO SAY THIS: that there's always more that can be said about Christ—always more that can be preached, more that can be taught and explicitly said. And it should all be preached and taught and explicitly said. But not without this quiet sign of Him, not without the thing we say by just being here.

What I've seen is a generation that wants to preach and teach the gospel to people who we've made it perfectly clear we don't want to look at or be around or enjoy.

Hospitality is not the same as good news. Hospitality cannot save. But it is our sign that this news is true. And without it we must wonder if we've really announced good news at all. Whatever we explicitly say of Christ must accompany this quiet sign of Him.

I was trained as a pastor, and every now and then I preach and teach at my job. But more often than not my job is to hear good news and just be out here. More often than not I'm just visiting. Out here visiting people whose world has ended. Setting a table at the end of the world. And saying what we say by just sitting here: that this end is not final, that the news is still true.

Out here just as a sign of this Person. Only a raggedy sign of His rest: this Person who alone *is* rest, rest from pride and lies, trouble and loss, chaos and disaster. Who is rest from all we've lost and all the lies we've been told and all the trouble we're in. And from the pride that's been our only shepherd.

Cleansed by this news, presented as this offering. Because the only thing left when the world ends is what we offer. Out here where there's nothing left but who we are at His table. Nothing left but the offer of bread and the holding out of light. Nothing left but rest.

A journey toward what we offer is a journey toward joy and rest. For me, a journey from pastor to chaplain. For all of us, a journey from helpless sinner to honored guest and humble servant. A journey that begins as we sit at His table and ends as we learn to serve it. A journey that isn't over until Christ comes back.

A journey toward wasted time. A journey toward what it means to serve.

And I begin with this. I begin with the work I do now. I begin with just sitting here.

I WORK FOR AN ECUMENICAL CHRISTIAN OUTREACH. We are an order of chaplain evangelists called to offer the ministry of presence to the world as it is and people as they are, to baffled old men smoking the world's cheapest cigarettes. We've been asked to love people who won't get better and to visit the people the worst has happened to.

It took a while to think of myself that way, as that chaplain, when I thought all I wanted to be was a pastor. There is a lot of overlap in the work, but the difference I've found is this: A chaplain visits. A chaplain is just with folks. A chaplain's job is to have time. Pastors do this, too, but pastors are in charge of churches, and a chaplain is in charge of nothing.

A chaplain is a ragged, stumbling sign of the Person this is all about. A lanky, lumbering, ragged, dusty, wobbly, decrepit, decomposing sign of the reality of Christ, the forgiveness of sins and the homecoming offered only in Him. He or she offers only those most basic, tender, and visible sign that this news is true: regard. And he or she offers this sign by just being here, by just visiting the people the worst has happened to. To go do this and share in Christ together, even if it's something awful.

People are on a long journey out of pride and lies, through trouble and loss, toward meaning and rest. It is a walk they take with Christ—the Christ who is their companion, their way out of pride and lies, through trouble and loss, meaning and rest their headed toward. He is their companion and a chaplain just a sign of His company. A chaplain is a good haunted house.

A chaplain offers presence always, and counsel only when wanted or needed. I talk about God all the time, but I don't often bring Him up. And people bring Him up often but only when and if they want to. I walk around a lot, but I only approach people I already know and I only talk about what they want to talk about.

Chaplains visit people, and this visiting is called the ministry of presence, a ministry made up of these three things: the regard we give, the company we keep, and the places of rest we make.

We talk about Jesus all the time, but first we offer the gift of regard: our most tender and visible sign of the reality of Christ, the forgiveness of sins, and the homecoming offered only in Him. The tender, stubborn light of this regard.

The tender stubborn light of regard is our primary offering, the primary gift to the people we visit, our gift to the world as it is, to people as they are. We offer it to all the crusty locals and all the baffling old men on stoops, but especially to the unwanted and the most vulnerable, turning our faces to the people the world has turned its face from. Our intention is to honor, uphold, and welcome the crushed by giving this regard. Regard is the offer of bread, the shining of light. It is our table at the end of the world.

Our intention is go see Grandma, when Grandma is a mean old man out on a stoop, when Grandma is sad and old and not doing well, or in prison, or in a psych ward.

To go and see them in the places where they do their sitting and their eating and their living and their dying, to go see them in the places where they won't get better and to offer this one small quiet sign of Him, to offer this one small thing by which Christ gathers them to Himself.

Because I believe there is something worse than all we've lost and all the trouble we're in and all the lies we've been told—and that is when it doesn't matter to you, or to anyone else.

Most of this wasted time is waiting for people to talk, waiting for them to say what they need to say, and only if they want to say it. And sometimes you have to wait on folks a while. Their world is foggy and spinning, their brains need a while to even begin to get the words for what's happening to them.

I go see an older special needs man in a care home. I say very little and wait to see if he wants to talk. It can take forever. He wants me there and his eyes light up, but he doesn't like questions. And so I sit and wait.

Once he took a good long look at me. His filmy eyes took on a fierce light. He put his hand firmly on the wooden tray table and shook the stuff that was on it.

"I'm here," he said. And pointed at a thumb at himself. "And I need the body and blood of Christ..."

He paused and let the words become a sentence in his head. And then again, with those clear bright eyes:

"...for my soul."

It was clear. He wanted *that* sign of Christ. He was a baptized Christian and he wanted communion. He wanted this sign of Christ. Words seem too painful and confusing to him. When you talk he shuts his eyes like its actually painful to hear you. He can't handle that much talk about anything at all. And so he needs this quiet sign of Christ instead. This visible grace. This offer of bread, this shining of light.

Many people don't take communion and don't want to talk religion. And yet they do want a visit. And the places to visit them are where you can almost feel all they've lost and all trouble they're in. We must go in with some sign of Him, some sign of the rest only He can bring. We must go in with some sign of Him, even if the only sign of Him is this regard. This strange sign that this news is true.

This regard: this tender stubborn light, the smallest, strangest sign of Christ. There's always more to say about Christ, but not without this quiet sign of Him.

What is regard? It is neither avoidance nor attack, but an offering. It is neither avoidance nor advance, but standing still. It is neither agreement nor disagreement, but a gift. It cannot be demanded, or it would not be a gift; it cannot be handed over in fear, or it would not be an offering. It cannot be bartered or bargained for, or it would be a commodity; it cannot be earned, or it would be a prize. It is only regard if it's offered. It is only offered if it's offered in His name, as a sign of the Person this is all about: the smallest, strangest sign of Him.

Regard is sustained, considerate attention. It is the very literal act of turning our face toward people. It is the tender acknowledgement of the reality of those made in His image. It is the look on your face that says the person in front of you matters and that it matters what they think and that it matters how they feel and that it matters what happens to them, given only in His name and only as a sign of Him. Because it is too tender and awful and baffling a thing to be given for any other reason.

Christ is bread and light; regard is the offer of that bread and the shining of that light, the strangest sign that this news is true. And I know it reveals Him somehow.

I know: the light is when He gave Himself. And the light is when we go and see each other.

Writing this book has the been the anguish of finding the words for exactly how it is a sign of Him, how it reveals Him, and how I found this quiet sign of Him in such a wild country.

I think of it like this: that Jesus Christ is God's face turned toward us. That He is God's welcome, He is our homecoming.

He is our rest from pride and lies, trouble and loss, chaos and disaster. That Christ was God reconciling the world to Himself. And I think of the cross as the full glory of that reconciliation, the full glory of that Face turned us, the fullest revelation of that regard. So that the power of Christ is the power of His cross.

The cross that is His gentleness, grief, and gladness all at once. The cross that is His joy, because His joy is to have us back. Regard is our sign of that cross. Regard is our crucifixion. And it is our share in the joy of return.

Regard is not bread and light. It does not save. It is not the feast; only Jesus is. But regard is the quiet offer of that bread and the quiet shining of that light. It is a kind of revelation of Christ. It is the revelation of Christ to the wounded soul and the hardened heart. It announces the Person this is all about.

I think about it this way: To give regard is to be given in His name, and to be given to His joy, as we give a more Ordinary Hospitality.

And this is not theoretical. It is practical. It is what five years as a kinda sorta chaplain has taught me. It's what this time out here has taught me, the little bit I've learned from all the time I've spent learning how to be with people again.

Out here on this stoop. Out here at His feast. Learning how to finally be with people again, to finally be with His people again. How to look at them, to treat them well, and to want to be around them. How to look at them and share in something and see them clearly. The joy we offer and the joy in offering.

THE OPPOSITE OF REGARD is disregard: the cold shoulder, the dismissive tone, the disqualifying remark, the haughty glance, the turned-up nose, the face we turn away from others.

The opposite of regard is hostility and refusal and contempt.

Its opposite is vengeance and retaliation. Its opposite is lashing out, striking back, getting back, getting even. It seems like most of what we offer is vengeance.

Regard is the painful renunciation of those things. It is the painful renunciation of our most basic instinct: to defend ourselves, take things back, and make things right. The painful renunciation of vengeance, retaliation, hostility, and spite toward others and toward ourselves. The painful renunciation of coercion and force and avoidance and condescension. The painful renunciation of our profound desire to turn our face away.

Regard is the quiet sign of Him. It is given in His name and it announces the Person this is all about, offered to the world as it is and people as they are, to the situation as it stands and the moments that we're in. This offer of bread, this shining of light. The most basic tender and visible sign of the reality of Christ, the forgiveness of sins, and the homecoming offered only in Him.

And the thing that makes it so hard is this: this gift, this offering, this regard *makes nothing right.* It is the crucifixion of making things better, the painful renunciation of making things right. It is only a sign that Christ has made things right. It is only a stained-glass window the light of Christ pours through.

It is only the smallest, strangest sign of Christ Himself. Regard means there's nothing to fix. Regard means there's nothing left but sharing in who He is and what He's done, nothing left but who we are at His table. Nothing but the offer of bread and the shining of light. Nothing but rest.

That's what I think now. When I think about this life, it seems there are no answers to be had, no sense to be made in this place of pride and lies, trouble and loss, chaos and disaster. And regard never has an answer. Regard just says there is still a Person in this place, this place where the worst happens and nothing makes sense and everything falls apart. There is still a Person this is all about. Regard is just a sign that this news is true. The light is when He gave Himself; the light is when we go and see each other. To go do this and share in Christ together.

Seen in this way, regard is always worthless, practically speaking. It is wasted time and it fixes nothing. And yet wasted time is the only way anything gets done. Everything I do as a part-time chaplain is based in this regard and in the strange power of this sign.

Everything our ministry has built has been built on this regard, this radiance, the offer of this bread, the shining of this light, this look, this revelation to the wounded soul and the hardened heart, this announcement of Him. The strangest sign of the Person this is all about.

And precisely because it fixes nothing and makes nothing right, precisely because it is only a sign, regard is always the place to begin again. It's the gentleness close at hand. It's what's left when there's nothing left. We fix nothing. We admit we only share in who He is and what He's done. We only give this and it is only given in His name. We only offer this tender, basic, and visible sign of the forgiveness of sins, the reality of Christ, and the homecoming offered only in Him.

We fix nothing because regard is, itself, something.

It casts its own bright light, strikes its own deep note of rest. It has its own stench. It is its own arrival at something. And it has its own glory: this offering, the blurring of this life into the world to come. It is its own word about that Word. It is its own sign that this news is true.

When we only offer regard, we've still offered something. When we offer anything without it, we haven't offered anything at all.

To give regard is to be given in His name and given to His joy, as we give a more Ordinary Hospitality. It is to learn His gentleness, enter His grief, share His gladness—the gentleness, grief, and gladness that is His cross. The cross that is also His joy. Because His joy is to have us back.

THE FIRST MEMOIR I WROTE, *A Quiet Mind to Suffer With*, was about trusting in Christ, trusting in His Word of mercy to us. Specifically, it was about trusting Him with the symptoms of a mental illness. It was about how I began to understand that illness as an affliction coming toward me rather than something deeply wrong with me or a reason to hate myself. It was about how I began to understand Jesus as the one who walks with us through every affliction.

If the first memoir was about trusting in Christ, this memoir—a sequel of sorts, or maybe just its companion—is about the regard we give to others, and especially that "other" other, which is always ourself.

Together, these two memoirs form my map of the five years that a would-be pastor spent learning to be a part-time chaplain. The first was about the things going on in my head; the second is about the things going on in my world.

The first, about my trust in Christ, was a lot easier to write. I was describing my interior life, my mental torment and my trust in Christ. I was describing what it felt like to have a mental illness. And I felt free to describe my mental illness. It felt like the only thing I could get wrong was myself.

This one, about regard for others, has been a lot harder. I'm describing other people: what I've done to them and what they've done to me and what I think about what they've done to me.

But as I wrote the first book I knew I needed the second. The picture of my mental collapse was not complete without a story of what other people had done to me. The picture was not complete without the disregard I'd been shown, without the abuse of a pastor, the neglect of a denomination, the alienation of a movement. And as I came out of that collapse with a patient quiet trust in Christ, I would come out of that abuse with a tender, stubborn regard for others.

And so these two books tell the story of those five years. A memoir about a quiet trust in Christ and a memoir about a tender, stubborn regard for others. And perhaps, unsurprisingly, about the habits that establish the first and prepare us for the second. Because I don't think love of God is possible without trust in Christ and I don't think love of neighbor is possible without regard for them.

In both books I come to this: that we love God and love our neighbor only as we trust in Christ. And we trust in Christ only by His gospel.

Both books tell the story of the only rest I've found: hearing the gospel and offering myself to the world as it is. The only rest I've found is hearing good news and just being out here, cleansed and presented by this good news, presented as an offering. All through His Spirit, and all of it a mending.

And so I'm on a lot of stoops and benches and dirty smelly hospital rooms, out giving this regard any way I can. I do a lot of sitting, a lot of visiting. Sometimes praying with folks, sometimes sharing Scripture. Sometimes bringing communion. But always this regard—always, always, always this quiet sign of Christ.

The ministry of presence is also called "porch light evangelism" and "rocking chair outreach." The feast is where the Word is preached and the Lord's Supper given in the fellowship of believers. But this is our porch light, our rocking chair, our invitation to the feast. I don't push people back to church, but when they find out what church I'm with a lot of them make their way here.

This is our song, the song by which Christ gathers His people to Himself. Our sign of His cross. Our sign of the reality of Christ, the forgiveness of sins, and the homecoming offered only in Him.

There's been times on this stoop when I've not been entirely sure the person across from me wasn't about to punch me in the face. And yet the Holy Spirit cleanses me with this news and presents me on this stoop. And cleansing and the presenting has been the mending of things far worse than a punch in the face. Things like just how hurt, scared, and upset I was when a pastor abused me and a denomination abandoned me. Things like that.

Until the world ends, this is where I'll be. This is what I'll be doing. I'll be busy wasting time. Out here giving regard. Waiting for people to say what they need to say, and only if they want to say it.

We go out and see people where they are, in the places where they do their sitting and their eating and their living and their dying, and this regard is our song to them. Our most tender, basic, and visible sign of the reality of Christ, the forgiveness of sins, and the homecoming offered only in Him. Offered to people as they are, the world as it is, the situation as it stands, and the moments we find ourselves in. Offered to baffled old men, to people who might just punch us in the face. This regard: our war on sin and death, our invasion of the present evil age.

It is an invasion because we don't just invite people into hospitality. We go out into the world with it, offering it to the world as it is, people as they are, the situation as it stands.

This regard, this gift, is a deep mystery to me. Its durability is even more mysterious. Regard is the impossible possibility, a revelation to the one who gives it and the one who receives it. Our sign of His cross. Our most basic, tender, and visible sign of the reality of Christ, the forgiveness of sins, and the homecoming offered only in Him.

We offer this regard and we behold what regard becomes. What have I seen, out on this stoop and everywhere else?

That if regard is a gift, then company is its vindication. The regard we give becomes the company we keep. And if regard is the gift and company is its vindication, then places of rest are its fulfillment. The regard we give and company we keep becomes these places of rest we've made. Real places of rest: real places with real chairs and real music and real bad coffee. Real third spaces: warped, ragged, crumbly signs of the forgiveness of sins, the reality of Christ, and the homecoming offered only in Him. Fragile, durable signs of rest.

Our ministry offers regard, company, and places of rest to the world as it is and people as they are. We offer regard always, but we only offer company and places of rest if they are welcome and wanted.

But often enough, people want the regard we give, the company we keep, and the places of rest we make. They are hungry for any genuine sign of goodness.

The regard we give and the company we keep become these weird third spaces, strange places for people to be and gentler ways for us to be together. Places where people somehow know they are welcome and enjoyed and where they know they are not going to be used, degraded, pushed, or devoured. Ways to be together that are not condescending or daunting, that neither ask too much or offer nothing at all. That are high welcome and low commitment. A place to be when there is nowhere to be. This place where we meet. This way to be together. This place we are all supposed to be. Our sign of His cross, our share in His joy.

Regard, company, and places of rest are our word about the Word, our invitation to His table, the radiance of this light, the song about His feast. Our quiet sign of Him. A welcome without words.

A place of rest because that is what they are most looking for: people who are hurting, dealing with things beyond them and beyond any words they have. And what they don't even have words to say is that they want a place of rest. A way to be okay and a sign they will be okay. And so before we even know what words to use, we must use this quiet sign of Him, this regard, this company, these places of rest.

We must have gentle, quiet signs of Christ to serve people whose lives are only chaos, who don't have words for all they've lost, all the trouble they're in, and all the lies they've been told, all the things coming toward them or all the things going on inside them. Contending with forces that have destroyed the words they might have had.

The people I know are in a place without words and they have no trust in the words we use. And so I think these quiet signs of

Christ are how we start again. Regard must be our first word, our first word about this Word. We begin with the ministry of presence. Just as Christ began with presence on the road to Emmaus, simply coming alongside the disciples and greeting them before anything was ever said.

It sounds ordinary because it is. The ministry of presence, this fierce song is *Ordinary Hospitality*. Except that the order is reversed: We don't invite people into it. We go out into the world with it as our most basic, tender, and visible sign of Him. It is not the innermost sanctum. It is the tip of the spear.

Regard doesn't save people; good news does. But regard is our most tender, basic, and visible sign that this news is true, that nothing that happens can change what life's about.

Ordinary Hospitality is our longing and sorrow. Our sign of the cross, our share in His joy. The place of anguish and light. To go see each other. To go do this and share in Christ together, even if it's something awful.

Uno and coffee can be a vindication of the good news, our sign that this news is true. It can be as ordinary and sad as a game of Uno and a cup of coffee. As ordinary and clumsy and sad and crumbly and mystical and baffling and Christ-haunted as Uno and a cup of coffee. This is the way we share in something and see each other clearly. The joy we offer, the joy in offering. The One we share in when we share something like this. A life in Christ that includes me seeing them and them seeing me.

And so what we do is very ordinary, but it is an ordinary thing in a sad place. An ordinary thing at the end of the world, at the very heart of all they've lost, all the trouble they're in, and all the lies they've been told.

These ordinary things, in this in this present evil age—in the land of sin, death, and the devil, this place of pride and lies, trouble and loss, chaos and disaster—are a magnificent obstinate grace, an invasion. In difficult places, ordinary things are a revelation. Ordinary Hospitality is a miracle. Ordinary Hospitality is the revelation of Christ to the wounded soul and the hardened heart.

Ordinary Hospitality: our most tender, basic, and visible sign of the reality of Christ, the forgiveness of sins, and the homecoming offered only in Him. Ordinary Hospitality: how we learn His gentleness, enter His grief, and share His gladness. Ordinary Hospitality: our strangest sign this news is true.

The regard we give, the announcement that Christ has died.

The company we keep, the announcement that Christ is risen.

These places of rest, the announcement that Christ will come again.

The thing we say by just being here: that Christ has died, Christ is risen, and Christ will come again.

We call these places of rest "outposts of creative hospitality," or "tables in the wilderness." These places for people to be, this gentler way to be together. Places they are supposed to be. They are our invitation to His table, our sign of the Person this is all about. A word about a Word, a more Ordinary Hospitality.

And I believe that you and me and everyone we know are only held together by those few good words about this Word. We are changed by good news and the few small signs that this news is true. We are gathered back, put back together by a few good words about this Word.

And it must be a gentle word about this Word. The folks who come to these spaces have been hurt. They've been crushed by others. Direct conversation, eye to eye contact, is too hard—too intense, too much. Questions feel like interrogation. They feel pushed aside by the words we use. Or else the words we use feel like snares and threats. And so there has to be something that's not just talking or looking at each other. We have to find some other way to be together, a gentler way to be together.

And the gentler way to be together is Uno, gel pens, music, donuts, coffee. This regard and company: these quiet signs of Christ. This gentler way to say this news is true: music so they don't feel like they have to talk. Local donuts and cheap Styrofoam cups that feel unpretentious and grounded in what is familiar. Uno because everyone knows how to play Uno, or can be taught how. Coffee because everyone drinks coffee. Music because most people like music. Sad folk music so people know not to get too excited. A gentleness close at hand. Things that are familiar. Some small sign of Him. A way to be together that doesn't feel like being completely exposed.

We do not do overt evangelism in these sanctuary spaces. We don't even play Christian music in the background. We haven't done much more than pray at mealtime and tell people what time church starts and that we can always help them with a ride. Still, many of the people we've met and sat with and played Uno with have come back to church. Most of them were already Christians. A more Ordinary Hospitality, from what I've seen, has brought them back, has been their return to the preached Word and the Lord's Supper in the fellowship of believers. Regard is the song by which Christ gathers His people to Himself, to Himself more fully revealed in the preached Word and the Lord's Supper.

So although there's no overt evangelism, building trust and establishing regard is, it seems, a kind of evangelism. It is simply the slowest kind, the one that looks the most like wasted time.

But it speaks of Christ, and folks come back and hear an explicit gospel they've already seen some strange sign of.

I see it on Sundays: a long procession of people we've met at care homes and soup kitchens lining up for the Lord's Supper after sitting under the preached Word.

And I laugh to think of how we all got here: so much Uno, so many gel pens, so much coffee, so much wasted time.

So much wasted time. So much wasted time. The incarnate funk of wasted time. The simple joy of wasted time. Just being here, just visiting.

And yet, to see them lining up with everyone else for the body and blood, lining up for Him and this feast, wasted time seems like the only thing that wasn't a waste of time. Wasted time seems like the shining of a light and the offer of this bread. Wasted time has a kind of radiance.

The smudge of glory, this life blurring to the world to come. The stench of beauty, goodness, and truth.

There is stained glass all around the sanctuary as they line up for the Lord's Supper. I think of all the men on our stoop lining up for it. I think of all of them and of all that stained glass.

The light is when He gave Himself; and the light is when we go and see each other. The light of the Christ pouring in through the stained-glass window of wasted time. Nothing left to do, nothing left but to share in who He is and what He's done by just being here. When there's nothing left but who we are this table. Nothing left but the offer of bread and the shining of light. Nothing left but rest.

And I think of myself there with them, getting in line too. Cleansed and presented by this good news, presented as this offering, and all through His Spirit and all of it a mending.

Learning, learning, learning, our song about His feast. The fierce song of wasted time. The fierce song of gentleness, grief, and gladness. Learning His gentleness, entering His grief, sharing His gladness.

This wasted time reveals His character. Especially when time is wasted on the people the world has turned its face from. Because wasted time is how Jesus gathers a people to Himself. Jesus will use Uno and coffee and gel pens to cast His light, make His character known, and gather a people to Himself.

He will use Uno and coffee and gel pens as a sign that this news is true.

Because people aren't coming back until they've been enjoyed. Until they feel safe. Until it matters what happened to them. Until we've played Uno with them.

I watch this long line of folks I know. The folks I've seen and loved on this stoop. And other folks, folks from care homes and folks just wandering round. Most of them already Christians.

How did they get back here? They got back here by being enjoyed.

There is no substitute for the preached Word and the Lord's Supper in the fellowship of believers. But if we want people to come to the Lord's Supper and the preached Word on Sunday we're going to have to play Uno with them on Friday, have coffee and play Uno with them in the places where they do their living and their grieving and their dying. We're going to have to find a gentler way to be together, without coercion or encouragement or pushing or persuading or bullying. We're going to have visit them when their world ends and set up a table at the end the world.

We're going to have play Uno with them as our invitation to that preached Word and our sign that this news is true. We need good news and we need to vindicate that good news by going to see each other.

But too often we have reserved Ordinary Hospitality only for those who have already returned to the preached Word and the Lord's Table. We have gone out into the world with preaching and teaching and withheld regard and company and places of rest. We have only offered hospitality to people who agree with us and who smell just fine.

I fear we have tried to tell people about Christ without offering this quiet sign of Him. I fear we have not only withheld regard, we have practiced disregard. We have tried to pastor a world without being its chaplain. We have tried to shepherd folks into His likeness that we don't ever want to see or be with or treat very well or enjoy at all. We have withheld our most basic and tender and visible sign of the reality of Christ.

The folks we've visited, the folks on the stoop, the folks just wandering around, come to our church on Sunday. I watch our door for them, because it's uncomfortable to walk into the places like church. It's a risk, an unknown, a threshold.

I see them at church on Sunday and I gently come up and tell them the bad coffee is almost ready. That I made it strong. Because if it's gonna be bad it better be strong. And I approach them with folding chairs in hand in case there's no room in the sanctuary so that we can make room anyway.

And what I'm trying to say: this is also a place of rest for them. Not just our temporary third space on Friday, but this place on Sunday. The preached Word and the Lord's Supper in the fellowship of believers is also a place of rest, from all they've lost, all the trouble they're in, all the lies they've been told. It is *the* place of rest. To show them they have moved from that small sign of rest to this deeper note of rest; that by coming on Sunday they have moved further and deeper into the only rest there is.

I used to feel weird about our folks on the street coming to church. Not just that they might be uncomfortable, but the nagging sense I have that when we do church we do something weird. Or cultish.

And that the folks will wonder: "Was that nice stoop guy just nice to me just to get me to do something weird like come to church with him?" Perhaps we all feel weird about sharing our faith.

And yet, over the years I've lost that odd feeling, or I have had to walk past it. Mostly because the gospel isn't a secret cult. The gospel is something that happened, it is *the thing* that happened: Christ's death, resurrection, and return. We have no need to fear an explicit gospel proclamation. It is an event in history. An event as visible and concrete as this strange sign that it is true: this more Ordinary Hospitality. The good news is a Person as visible and concrete as these strange signs of Him.

We do not have to fear people winding up at church. The gospel isn't self-help or indoctrination. The gospel is visible. A Person who died and rose again. And the Holy Spirit isn't always a mystery either. The Holy Spirit uses audible news of Him to gather a visible fellowship to Him.

And yet we have put such a burden on folks to share their faith only verbally, to go out and boldly proclaim it, that we have made people feel like they're not really Christians unless they're manipulative and rude, unless they direct vulnerable relationships toward canned talk that feels awkward and embarrassing—because it is. Because in those moments there really has been a violation of the trust established between friends. In order to tell this news we don't have to violate our most basic, tender, and visible sign that this news is true. We don't have to practice disregard.

When people think you're spending time with them to convert them, they feel cheap, cornered, and used. And they probably should.

It is okay to be friends with nonbelievers, to ask them questions that have nothing to do with digging into them or making them feel wounded and vulnerable so that they feel their need for Christ. And it is okay to not to suddenly confront them with Jesus on camping trips and coffee shops after being mysteriously nice to them for a few weeks.

It's also okay to tell people that Jesus means a lot to you, or that your faith is the only thing that gets you through the day. Or that you must do something or can't do something because you're a Christian. Or that your faith shapes your life choices in such and such a way or makes you see things in such and such a way. That is no violation of hospitality. That's just bearing witness.

But you don't have to convince anyone of anything. You don't have to be pushy and rude. You don't have to exploit the fragile trust you've established with others in order to corner them to Christ. Regard is its own sign of Christ. You can just give regard.

Be their friend and let them know you care about what happens to them. Give them regard and company in the hard spots they're in. When you're led to, tell them that you're a Christian and what Christ has meant to you. But stop forcing awkward questions on your friends because they trust you. It's okay to tell someone you're a Christian and then spend the rest of your life just caring about what happens to them.

What nonbelievers or lapsed Christians need is the preached Word and a more Ordinary Hospitality. They good news of Scripture and signs that this news is true. Stop cornering vulnerable people. Start gently inviting folks to church and let them know they can always come with you and you can always pick them up. And then just drop it.

We've put a great burden on laypeople to evangelize and share their faith, to the point that we don't think the Sunday sermon creates Christians, we think our personal testimony does. We think our canned talk and personal testimony creates Christians, that the preached Word encourages us, and that Ordinary Hospitality is how we encourage other Christians. And maybe it does, but is that how it all is supposed to go?

What have I seen? That Ordinary Hospitality builds trust and establishes regard and welcomes nonbelievers, that the preached Word creates believers, and that personal testimonies encourage other believers.

A more Ordinary Hospitality is our invitation to the Lord's Supper and the preached Word. And if they come, we trust the preached Word to do the work of creating saving faith. So that, when they come into contact with preached Word, they recognize, in the words about Him, the same Person they caught sight of when you gave them regard and came alongside them.

I can hear myself asking: But is that enough? Do people really come back that way? And all I have to say is: absolutely. All the time.

But it's the bums and the derelicts and crazies who come. The sad uglies and dirty smellies. Not that we should see them that way or refer to them that way, but we instinctively do. When you know their names they stop appearing that way to you and they're just people you know. Folks you care about.

But I can sense a secret fear in all of us. That if we do it this way, it's the sad uglies and the dirty smellies who will come back. Folks who aren't welcome anywhere and certainly aren't enjoyed once they're there. But who are the most in need of some sign of the reality of Christ, the forgiveness of sins, and the homecoming offered only in Him. Who would love to be invited anywhere, ever.

People come back to the preached Word and the Lord's Supper all the time. It just seems like it's never the shiny folks we want. It's the people the worst has happened to. The afflicted, the derelicts.

But I see the people the worst has happened to shuffling up to the Lord's Supper after the preached Word, and I know. Regard is the song by which Christ brings people back to His church. Regard, company, and places of rest have been their way back. It has been their gentle way back, a way back they take in their own way and in their own time.

I OFTEN THINK OF THIS GOOD NEWS. The confession of Christ as Lord and Savior. The announcement that Christ has died, Christ is risen, and Christ will come again. And the news that the forgiveness of sins and the gift of the Holy Spirit is now offered in His name.

I think of how this good news is not just information. How it is made living and active through the power of His Spirit and for the building of a fellowship. This good news is the light that reveals Him and the bread by which He gives Himself to us. How Jesus is the feast, but so is this good news. And I think of how this good news comes to us through the preached Word and the Lord's Supper.

I think of Christ as the Feast of Bread and Light, and the preached Word and the Lord's Supper in the fellowship of believers as the feast *right now.* I think of this good news as the feast right now: Christ with us by His gospel through His Spirit and for the building of His fellowship. And I think of Ordinary Hospitality as the radiance of that feast.

Hospitality doesn't save people; good news does. But hospitality is our most tender, basic, and visible sign that this news is true. It is the invitation for them to hear this news as true.

And I think of how a more Ordinary Hospitality *is* the foretaste of the riches of the preached Word and the Lord's Supper in the fellowship of believers. Of the Christ displayed there, more fully revealed there. It *is* the threshold, the open door to that fuller revelation. A more Ordinary Hospitality is the offer of bread and the shining of light. Our most tender, basic, visible sign of reality of Christ, the forgiveness of sins, and the homecoming offered only in Him. Offered to a world that has lost all words, that has no words for all the things coming toward them and all the things going on inside them, no words for all they've lost, all the trouble they're in, all the lies they've been told.

And for those folks, maybe these quiet signs are a place to start again.

And I think we must stand at the boundary of the present evil age of sin, death, and the devil, in this place of pride and lies, trouble and loss, and offer that radiance, this word about the Word, this sign that this news is true. We must make that invitation, sing that song. This fierce song, this obstinate grace, this tender stubborn regard. We must go out into the world with a more Ordinary Hospitality.

I think of the stoop. There's people smoking and then there's me sitting there. And there's smoke from those cigarettes and there's my scribbles on the pages. And there's the hot sun on all of us.

I think of how this stoop sits at the corner of our church, jutting out into the comings and goings of all these wounded, lovely, selfish people like me. Because someone's world is always ending, Ordinary Hospitality is always our table at the end of the world: this place of pride and lies, trouble and loss, chaos and disaster.

I sit on this stoop because there's nothing left but to share in who He is and what He's done. There's nothing but who we are at this table. Nothing but the offer of bread and the shining of light. Nothing left but rest. The only rest I've found: hearing good news and just being out here. Cleansed by this news and presented on this stoop. And all through His Spirit and all of it a mending.

Later, yes, catechism, Bible studies. All the facts of salvation. Things we don't have to be ashamed of because they actually happened and must be said. His death and resurrection as concrete and visible and strange as our signs that this news is true. So that we need not ever fear speaking of it. But not without this quiet sign of Him. And at least right now just this. At least right now just this quiet sign of Him. This word about the Word.

Like the pointed bow of a ship, the tip of the spear, a more Ordinary Hospitality, the invasion of the present evil age. An invading radiance. The fiercest song. The strangest sign.

Fierce song because it is a fierce thing to offer an obstinate grace, a tender stubborn regard. A fierce thing to learn His gentleness, enter His grief, and share His gladness. A fierce thing to be given to His joy when His joy is to have His people back. And when His people are a bitter feast.

Fierce because it's hard, strange because it doesn't make sense. The nonsense of saying that patience and longing are the sorrow. And that the sorrow is the joy, and that the joy is the joy of return.

The gentleness, grief, and gladness of all of it. The gentleness, grief, and gladness that is His cross. A cross that is also His joy. Because His joy is to have us back.

The fierce strange thing it all is. This regard. Our sign of His cross, our share in His joy. This anguish and light. This place we meet.

On Fridays our church becomes this fierce song, this place of rest, our strange sign that this news is true. On Friday we give regard, come alongside, and make a place for people to be. A place where they know they are welcome and enjoyed and know they are not going to be used, degraded, or devoured.

On Fridays our doors are open for four hours and we call it "Open Hours."

Open Hours is our weekly announcement of the Person this is all about, an announcement made with coffee, donuts, gel pens, music, and card tables: a coffeehouse with a very large arts and craft table. Sometimes, if the weather is nice, we put a table outside and make this announcement from the parking lot. A bunch of tables and coffee and gel pens. An obstinate grace, a tender, stubborn regard. We do it for the blessed stench of it, for the radiance of that light. Because bread is a good enough reason to hold out bread, and light is a good enough reason to offer light.

This place, this regard, is not agreement with the world, or friendship with the world, but always a friendship *toward* it. Always this offer to the world as it is, people as they are. Always this sign of Him, always the most tender basic visible sign of the reality of Christ, the forgiveness of sins, the homecoming offered only in Him.

Before the day starts, a few volunteers and a few crusty locals gather upstairs to do a liturgy made up of a simple confession of sin, short readings from Scripture, and set prayers. We do a short liturgy in a stuffy room. I tell people that a liturgy is just

Scripture organized for the scattered mind, and that we all need it because all our minds are scattered. We use little pocket-sized books I made by hand with rubber bands and folded sheets of computer paper. We sit in a small stuffy room above the noise of people slowly coming in. We sit down, make small talk, open a window, and do a short liturgy in a stuffy room.

With this liturgy, we slowly recite the words of Scripture. This liturgy is a gift from the denomination I left. I'm in a new church, a new denomination, but I've kept the same old liturgy. It was hard to leave my denomination. They gave me the things I love. Liturgy, rhythm, and song. They made Scripture sing to me.

The good news still comes to me through that liturgy, rhythm, and song. And I offer it to our volunteers before the third space begins. We hear the words of Scripture and liturgy makes that news come to us in gentle lapping waves. The gentle lapping waves of unchanging news. Unchanging news that continues to change us. This news: the light by which we see Him, the bread by which He gives Himself to us.

The Old Testament promises of a good king, a new heart, and a return home. The New Testament announcement that those promises are now fulfilled in Christ. This good news made living and active through His Spirit for the formation of a little group of people. A little group of people committed to the work of magnificent obstinate grace and tender stubborn regard. A little group of people who need to hear those promises.

We do a liturgy, a boring wonderful little ol' liturgy where the good news comes to us in gentle lapping waves. We do it to be cleansed by this news, presented as this offering. And all through His Spirit and all of it a mending.

This is what it seems like now: The preached Word and the Lord's Supper in the fellowship of believers is the feast right now. But the daily recitation and reflection on the words of Scripture *keeps the feast,* continues that feast. The good news, preached and shown on Sunday, is now rehearsed, recited, chewed on, dwelled on during the week. We sit with the unchanging news that continues to change us. We continue hearing this news, receiving this mercy, keeping this feast, even with just a boring ol' liturgy.

Lord and Savior. Died, risen, returning. The forgiveness of sins, the gift of the Holy Spirit. Wash, rinse, repeat. Is it repetitive? Of course. It has to be. It's news that hasn't changed since last time we heard it.

I've wondered whether we should do more than just a short liturgy in a stuffy room. But when you have a bunch of people of various backgrounds, understandings, and cognitive abilities, a short liturgy of Scripture and prayer is just about the only thing we can all do together. A short liturgy seems like the only feast we have right now. A way to share in something and see each other clearly. A way to hear good news and turn our face to each other. A life in Christ that includes me seeing them, them seeing me.

We gather in that stuffy room sitting over our third space. We recite the words of Scripture and say prayers. And then we commit ourselves to the mundane acts of service. That more

Ordinary Hospitality. Our song to the world as it is, people as they are. We heard good news and then go downstairs and give our sign that this news is true. Cleansed with this news, presented as this offering. And all through His Spirit and all of it a mending. This trust in Christ, this regard for others. And the Holy Spirit who makes it all possible, the One who makes it possible to believe in the gospel and somehow live as if it were true. The One who makes it possible to trust in Christ and present ourselves to God as those who have been brought from death to life.

The vindication of this good news: a long, slow walk with His Spirit, who leads us from hearing through prayer toward offering. A daily walk from Scripture through prayers to hospitality. This is the Simple Rhythm my life has become. A Simple Rhythm because I need it. A simple life with this good news. The long, slow walk with His Spirit.

My daily walk is made up of all those liturgies, songs, and rhythms my denomination gave me. That news coming to us in gentle, lapping waves through the liturgies, songs, and rhythms. Unchanging news that continues to change me.

We do a short liturgy in that stuffy room and then pull out the folding tables, the gel pens, the Uno cards. Our strange signs this news is true. We do a short liturgy and then get the donuts and put on the coffee. And then we sit at the tables we set up. And then we sit with the folks we got donuts for and put on coffee for.

Sometimes that seems like all my life is: a Simple Rhythm leading me to the fiercest song.

Trust in Christ leading to regard for others. Sometimes that seems like all there is: this good news, a more Ordinary Hospitality. Cleansed and presented by this good news. Presented as an offering. And all through His Spirit. And all of it a mending.

Cleansed as helpless sinners. Mended as honored guests. Presented as humble servants. Cleansed and presented by His gospel, through His Spirit, to His fellowship.

A simple life with this good news, so that wounded, selfish people can reveal Christ to wounded, selfish people. So that wounded, selfish people can be given to wounded, selfish people. So that wounded, selfish people can be given to His joy.

AND WE MUST BE PREPARED and cleansed and presented by His gospel and through His Spirit and to His fellowship, because you and I are awful and we love and serve an awful people.

People who are awful and more than just awful: awful and more mysterious than just awful, ruined gods, frightened children, complete strangers. Wounded, selfish people called to reveal Christ to wounded, selfish people.

This Simple Rhythm—this simple life with His news, the slow walk with His Spirit, the daily habits that establish that trust and prepare us for this regard—are essential because the work is hard and people are so wounded, so lovely, and so selfish, and so are we.

We must have this news come to us in gentle lapping waves. The unchanging news that continues to change us. Because other people are the bitter feast. And the bitter feast is Christ as well. Christ is there as well. He is One who's there whenever wounded, lovely, selfish people are given to wounded, lovely, selfish people. Somehow He is there, in all the anguish and light. In all this sorrow and gladness, Christ is there as well. There to cleanse and present us. To cleanse us with His news and present us and this offering. And all through His Spirit and all of it a mending.

He's the one who is given whenever we give regard. Our sign of His cross, our share in His joy. This anguish and light. This place we meet.

I have a real hard time doing this. Giving myself to the world as it is, to people as they are, to the moments that I'm in, to the situation as it stands. I have a hard time giving regard.

It is not just that it's hard to do, it's that I can't do it. It's that regard is impossible. It simply is not possible to give it.

It's not just that it's hard, it's that there is a revolt in me, a refusal in the deepest place, an unwillingness called myself. A refusal to give myself to others, the stubborn fact that I know what I should do and just don't want to do it. The ministry of presence is our gift to wounded, selfish people. It is our most basic, tender, and visible sign of Him. And I still cannot give it.

Sitting with wounded, lovely, selfish people and listening to wounded, lovely, selfish people and drinking coffee with wounded, lovely, selfish people can often feel worthless, pointless, stupid, and futile. It feels like I'm stuck or trapped and nothing's happening and that it's all just stupid and rotten and foul. And I'm seized with a sudden despair.

And the people. My goodness, the people: bitter, funny, contentious, defensive, volatile, petty, pouty. Brilliant, demanding. Pushy, grabby. Rough, compelling, utterly fascinating, completely uncooperative. Heinous, vile, and pretty great. And all their tender, ruthless, heartless, wild, wonderful talk. And the glory of their sad, tired faces.

And how can they be like this? Why can't they just be nice? And the answer is, they can't help it. The answer is, they cannot be gentle. The answer is, too much has happened for them to be any other way. The answer is all they've lost and all the trouble they're in and all the lies they've been told and the pride that's been their only shepherd.

The answer I have for them is the answer I have for me. I think of all of them. Opinionated, easily offended, controlling, oblivious, inconsiderate, spiteful. And beautiful and wonderful. Beautiful and horrible. Sacred and unacceptable.

Sitting at the bitter feast of others. Anguish and light. The bitter feast of all the crusty locals. Regard for all the crusty locals. And looking at myself in the mirror and seeing that I am the bitter feast as well.

Terrible, horrible, impossible. And wonderful, wonderful, wonderful. Ruined gods, frightened children, complete strangers. All these wounded, lovely, selfish people. And the glory of all our sad, tired faces.

And I cannot give myself to them. I cannot work with His joy. I cannot learn His gentleness and enter His grief and share His gladness. I cannot keep this feast.

I get stuck. Thwarted, vexed, stuck, blocked, trapped. And seized with sudden despair.

I get stuck and I don't know what this is all about. I don't know what this is all about if this is what life is going to be like.

Everyone here so wounded, lovely, and selfish. And you feel like all you have for them is vengeance, retaliation, hostility, and spite. And all you want to do is defend yourself. Take things back, make things right. All we have for each other is vengeance.

And all you have is the sweet cry for mercy. When the bitter feast is actually a furnace and the furnace is all the things they want and all the problems they have and how hurt and upset they are and how they will push and pull on you to get the things they want and solve all the problems they think they have and how they grip and shove to get what they want. When people are a furnace and you can only stand so close.

When a more Ordinary Hospitality is the only thing allowed in a furnace like that. When only regard can stand in that furnace. This strange sign of Him. When only the fiercest song sits for the bitter feast. The anguished cry of just hanging in there. The incarnate funk of just sitting there, just visiting.

This regard. This quiet sign of Him. This sign of His cross.

This sorrow and longing. This place of anguish and light. This place we meet.

And you know you cannot stand in that furnace. You know you cannot sit at that feast. You cannot give yourself to wounded, lovely, selfish people. You cannot be a sign of anything. Because it is not possible to calmly serve the ruined god, the frightened child, and the complete stranger.

It isn't just that it's impossible to be always charming and charismatic. It's impossible to just be steady, impossible to simply not react to their woundedness and selfishness. It's impossible to just not be hostile.

And yet we cannot ask the world to be a certain way before we're willing to serve it, to reveal Christ to it. Or else revelation is not revelation. Or else there is no radiance and no announcement, no strange sign of Him, no strange sign of this gift we have in Christ. No strange sign of the Person this is all about. No quiet sign of Him, no word about this Word.

And that is where we are stuck. We cannot give ourselves to others and we cannot ask them to be any other way before we're willing to serve them.

And maybe that is the point about serving: You begin to see that it has very little to do with who you are or who they are. It has a lot more to do with who He is and what He's done. That other people aren't a good enough reason to do anything. That only mercy is. Bread is the only reason we hold out bread. Light is the only reason we offer light.

That there's nothing left to do, nothing left but share in who He is and what He's done. When there's nothing but who we are at this table. Nothing left but the offer of bread and the shining of light. Nothing left but rest. To share in it so we might be cleansed and presented. All at once by His dying and rising. Day by day as we hear good news and offer a more Ordinary Hospitality.

You are forced to see that serving is never about how terrible or great the people you're serving are. Serving is about the Person it announces. And what He's like. And the fellowship that He's building.

You are forced to see that regard is only regard if it is offered in His name. That is too awful and baffling to be a thing to be given for any other reason.

And maybe that is what we learn: that ministry really isn't possible. And maybe that is the purpose of getting stuck, of feeling blocked and being trapped, of being seized with a sudden despair: to learn, again and again, that when it comes to this ministry of presence, that when it comes to being a chaplain or anything at all in His name, that the way is blocked except for Christ's own life, except for the reality of His death and resurrection and our share in it by this good news. That there is no way past this thing called myself except by His death and resurrection. That we are cleansed and presented all at once by His dying and rising and day by day as we hear this news and offer a more Ordinary Hospitality.

That is all there is. And still, even in the anguish, the only rest I've ever known: hearing good news and just being out here. To be cleansed by this news, and presented as this offering. And all through His Spirit and all of it a mending. Good news that wants to rescue our trust in Him, shepherd our attention toward Him, and give us to each other in Him, so that we can give regard, come alongside, and make this place of rest.

Working with His joy, we are made ready for that joy. Working with His joy, we are given to this joy. We keep this feast. We share in that joy and are made joyful.

To give regard, and be given in His name and be given to His joy, as we give a more Ordinary Hospitality. This regard: our sign of His cross and our share in His joy.

I think that's it, really: to give regard, and be given in His name, and be given to His joy, is to share in His joy and see Him more clearly. Seeing Him more clearly, we only want to see Him more clearly.

And so I serve Him not to please Him, or not merely to please Him, but to see Him more clearly.

I give regard, and am given in His name, and given in His joy, to see Him more clearly.

This regard, this sign of His cross, is anguish. But I cope with that anguish because it is an anguish that still seeks the face of Christ. This anguish is still the color blue. This anguish is still longing and sorrow and gladness. It is still light. I cope with this anguish because there's still nothing left but to share in who He is and what He's done.

THE GOSPEL WANTS TO GIVE US BACK TO GOD, ourselves, and each other. It's the gospel's job; it is what the gospel wants to do. And it is His Spirit who makes sure it happens, who makes sure we hear this news, have this bread, see this light, receive this mercy, behold this Person. And keep this feast.

A feast that changes what we want. That is the power of the cross as I understand it, the power of the gospel: the power to change what we trust so that we trust in Him instead. To trust in Him instead of pride and lies. Which matters because what we trust changes what we pay attention to. And what we pay attention to changes what we want.

That is what I think it means to share in who He is and what He's done. What it means to be cleansed by this news and presented as this offering. For Him to change what we trust, pay attention to, and even want.

So that what we want is to be rescued by His gospel and die with Him. To be led through His Spirit and rise with Him, to be given to His fellowship and share in the joy of His return.

And what a painful thing it is to believe in that cross, to keep this feast, to be given by Christ to others. What a painful thing it is to see Him clearly. What a painful thing that freedom is, when what we want is freedom from suffering and what He offers is freedom from pride and lies.

The painful cleansing of a hardened heart, the painful mending of our wounded soul, and the anguished presentation of ourselves at the bitter feast.

As we become a strange sign that this news is true. As we become the strangest sign of this good news, a strange sign called more Ordinary Hospitality.

THIS CHANGE IN WHAT WE TRUST, pay attention to, and even want is what I call a Crucified Heart. It is one of the other things I believe in; it's also called *faith, hope, and love*. It is our deeper trust in Him by the power of His gospel.

I'll sit on the stoop and draw that Crucified Heart on stray pieces of paper all the time. I draw a Crucified Heart sitting on the stoop with all my gel pens. What I draw is this: a stupid heart like one a child would draw, with a cross piercing the center of it like a fish hook so that it makes a wound. But the wound is also shining. The heart is pierced but the pierced heart is shining, because the pierced heart is a new heart of faith, hope, and love.

I call it a Crucified Heart because of how painful it is. How painful it is for our trust to be rescued, our attention to be led, for our selves to be given. How painful it is to be given in His name, given to His joy, and see Him clearly. How painful to be cleansed with this news, presented as this offering. And all through His Spirit and all of it a mending.

How painful it is to be given back by good news. News that cannot change but that continues to change us.

How painful it is to be changed by His joy, for His joy to change what we want most. How painful it is to want something more than pleasure and pain. How painful it is to want something else more than what you want most. How painful it is to eat this bread and see this light, hear this news, receive this mercy, behold this Person. How painful it is to be cleansed and presented. All at once by His dying and rising. Day by day as we hear this news and offer a more Ordinary Hospitality.

How painful it is to become rescued, led, and given in this place where the worst happens and nothing makes sense and everything falls apart.

I need a Crucified Heart to get anything done. I need a Crucified Heart to just be here. To even be a part-time chaplain. To head toward the only kind that has ever struck that deeper note of rest. A Crucified Heart: wounded, shining, bright.

And I need a Simple Rhythm to get that Crucified Heart. A slow walk with His Spirit, a simple life with this good news. To be rescued by His gospel and die with Him. To be led through His Spirit and rise with Him. To be given to His fellowship and share in the joy of His return.

A Simple Rhythm, the fiercest song. This good news, a more Ordinary Hospitality. The feast right now.

THIS BOOK, I'VE SAID, IS A JOURNEY toward what it means to serve His table. A journey through confusion and pain until I arrived at just sitting here.

Out here on this stoop. A journey toward wasted time. Toward the incarnate funk of just being here. Toward the only kind of life that ever struck that deeper note of rest. Toward hearing good news and just being here. Toward the blessed stench, the smudge of glory: this life blurring to the world to come.

A journey toward giving regard. Toward being given in His name, given to His joy. Seeing Him more clearly as I give a more Ordinary Hospitality.

The question this memoir asks is this: But is there really something life's about? Is there really a Person this is all about? Is there actually something to want more than pleasure or pain? Is there really something else to want most?

Is there really a Word, a feast, that will give us back to ourselves? That can change what we want most?

And can we really become a word about that Word, a song about that feast? A sign that this is all true?

Is our regard really our most basic tender and visible sign of the reality of Christ, the forgiveness of sins, and the homecoming offered only in Him?

And is it true that His cross is His joy, because His joy is to have His people back? Is it really possible for Him to change what we want so that what we want most is to work with His joy? So that what we want most is to be rescued by His gospel and die with Him, to be led by His Spirit and rise with Him, to be given to His fellowship and share in the joy of His return?

What I mean is, can we be cleansed and presented? Can He change what I trust, pay attention to, and even want? I don't always know. But I know we cannot make ourselves want something we do not want. We can go ahead and try, but it will only make everything worse.

All I can do is have a simple life with this good news. A slow walk with His Spirit. A Simple Rhythm of Scriptures, prayers, and service. Good news coming to me in gentle, lapping waves. Through Scripture, through rhythm, liturgy, and song. Good news that cannot change but continues to change me.

Good news that wants to change what we trust, pay attention to, and even want. And all through His Spirit and all of it a mending. A Simple Rhythm, a simple life, a slow walk to crucify the heart more, so that the wound gets deeper and brighter. So that out of that heart comes this blessed stench.

A JOURNEY THAT STARTED AFTER I'D BEEN CRUSHED by a mentor, abandoned by a denomination, alienated from a movement. After the church betrayed my trust, and after it did what it should not have done. After I crashed and burned on an idea of myself as a pastor.

What was the pastor guilty of? Spiritual abuse. What was the denomination guilty of? Simple neglect of duty. What did that movement do? Became hostile to the world, practiced disregard, and punished people for not being Christian yet.

Crushed by people who love Jesus. And learning how to be with them again. The deep gladness of a wounded, lovely, selfish person given to wounded, lovely, selfish people. It has taken years. It will take the rest of my life.

But I know this: This work, the work of just sitting here, the work of a part-time chaplain, has been my reconciliation with orthodox Christianity.

For years after I'd been crushed, abandoned, and alienated, it didn't feel like there was such a thing as myself. I felt too crushed and selfish to be myself. Too crushed and selfish to be a person. Being a person involved too much pain. It felt like I'd disintegrated in this place of pride and lies, trouble and loss, chaos and disaster. Buried under all that rubble. And it didn't feel like I was there under all that rubble. I wasn't there under everything that happened to me. No way back to myself, no way to get myself back. And no way my life would have color or light or rest.

I look back on those years and ask what has meant the most. My life in that wild country. I ask myself what held me together.

Held together by Scripture and friendship. Trust in Christ and regard for others. A Simple Rhythm, the fiercest song, this good news, a more Ordinary Hospitality. Held together by the feast right now. Hearing good news and just being here, the only table I've found in this place, this place where the worst can happen and nothing makes sense and everything falls apart.

We are all looking for a life that won't fall apart. This is the only one I found. A life with this good news. Held together by a few good words about this Word. Held together by good news and a few good signs that this news is true.

Scripture and friendship. A Simple Rhythm, the fiercest song. This good news and a more Ordinary Hospitality. To get myself back. Cleansed and presented until I was myself again. Held together by the feast right now. The table in this place. Until I was myself again.

I realize, in doing this work, that I'm serving a church that did me wrong. A tradition that did me wrong. I work with denominations that have destroyed people I love, and crushed myself and others. It has hardened my heart, so that I feel like I cannot give myself to others. I feel like I cannot give myself to the same people who did this, the same kind of people who did this. I feel like this cannot be my feast. Not this, not the bitter feast of other people. Not after what they've done.

How can Christ be there as well? Is it true? That the bitter feast is Christ as well? That I can be given by Christ to others? Presented at the bitter feast of other people?

I think again of how serving is just an announcement. That regard only announces a Person and not vengeance or solutions. That regard is the cleansing and mending of two wounded, selfish people. The radiance of Christ to both: the one who sees and the one who's seen. The one who gives and the one who receives. Cleansed and mended as we are given by Christ to each other. That Christ is always at the bitter feast. The One who's there whenever wounded, lovely, selfish people are given to wounded, lovely, selfish people.

One day at Open Hours, when the weather was nice and the folding table was outside and Uno cards and gel pens were moving back and forth a little in the wind, an older man in our fellowship looked me in the eye and asked if he could go get his boom box, come back, and play Loretta Lynn. That was what he wanted to do. The gel pens. The Uno. The coffee. This gentle way to be together. It wasn't enough. What we needed was a boom box. What we needed was Loretta Lynn.

What I said was, "Of course."

This is not a man who shares much, who offers much. He is an older man with special needs, in his sixties. His big thing is kind of just staring into space. Every now and then he will turn around and make a joke before turning back to the vast emptiness he was staring at. Whatever other emotion will have briefly flashed across those blue eyes, his face will always return to the same standing frown, a bored, sour grimace: the look he hangs his face on. He and that look on his face are content to just sit there all day, surrounded by gel pens and music and coffee without drawing or drinking or really listening. But today his face had changed, and all he wanted was Loretta Lynn's gospel album.

This is not a man who likes to move. And it was hot out here and it was not a short walk over to where Loretta Lynn's gospel album was. But this was what he thought was really worth doing. It felt like a pilgrimage for him to do it. And he made it sound like everything would be different if he did.

So I said, "Yes."

He trudged off the parking lot where we sat, trudged off with that bored and sour look on his face, and thirty minutes later he was back with his boom box, that same sour look, and a collection of CDs. Thumbing through I found the Commodores, Shania Twain, Toby Keith, and Earth, Wind & Fire.

We spent a few minutes running out extension cords and getting his boom box plugged up. He found his Loretta Lynn gospel album and it played to a parking lot, played to the people coming and going on the street nearby. It played to people who had groceries to get, kids to raise, drugs to do.

People we knew, people we didn't know. Before long more people were sitting with us. And there was time, it seemed like, for lots of things. But mostly there was time to sit and talk about music: the Commodores, Shania Twain, Toby Keith, and Earth, Wind & Fire.

We were out here with all these wounded, lovely, selfish people. Ruined gods, frightened children, complete strangers. People who were not okay. But right now we were all okay, and this was the place we were supposed to be, honored guests of the weather outside and the Loretta Lynn gospel album. Every crushed and wonderful person. The glory of their sad and tired faces. An ease, a rapport. This small talk. This thing between us. Something to share in, partake of. This gentle way to be together. To share in something, and see each other clearly. The Person this is all about. The joy we offer, the joy in offering. The One we share in when we share something like this.

We had just done the Daily Office and come out with coffee, to visit each other, to see each other, to be out here with the Loretta Lynn and the rest of the world.

The boom box was here. Loretta Lynn's voice was with us. The Lord was with us. And this was our place of rest. And there was a table out here, in the midst of all we'd lost and the all the trouble we're in and all the lies we'd been told. A table in this place of pride and lies, trouble and loss, chaos and disaster.

There was a table here, quite literally here in this parking lot. And I got to see people being themselves again. And that was the delight. To be there when ruined gods, frightened children, and complete strangers became themselves again, were cleansed and presented and become themselves again, even if just for a little while. When there is a feast right now. A place we're supposed be. When everyone is an honored guest and humble servant for just a little while.

I think of how something so stupid can do so much. How something as foolish and stupid as boom box could give us back to ourselves, and each other.

At moments like this, at tables like this, I feel like I almost understand myself, I am on the cusp of the only thing my life's about. That simple goodness we all feel when there's finally something life's about. A Person this is all about. Even in the midst of all we've lost and all the trouble we're in and all the lies we'd been told.

The deep gladness of just being here, and seeing other people clearly.

Sitting here, being friends, hearing promises. Held together by the feast right now. When there's nothing left to do, nothing but to share in who He is and what He's done. Nothing but trust in Christ and regard for others. Scripture and friendship. Good news and Ordinary Hospitality.

I don't know whether, a year ago, I could have accepted the offer to sit at the table. To see Him this clearly, to see this as a sign of Him, as a sign that this news is true. To see this as our most basic tender and visible sign of the reality of Christ, the forgiveness of sins, and the homecoming offered only in Him.

The light of Christ pouring in through the stained-glass window of wasted time. This sign of His cross, this share in His joy. The anguish and light. The foul, blessed stench, the unbearable, glorious smudge: this life blurring to the world to come. The song about His feast. The radiance of that light, a word about that Word. Sitting here, being friends, hearing promises.

It has been my intuition all my life that, in the midst of all the things I wanted, there must be something else to want most. Something else that this was all about. Something to love more than pleasure or pain. Some other joy and some better feast. I remember thinking there must be a way toward this, toward this thing to most want. To be given back to what I wanted. A way to move toward what I was supposed to want most. A journey toward a better feast.

And what did I have now? With these people, this boom box? I had a brief moment where I knew what I wanted. I wanted that better feast. I wanted that better longing. I wanted the thing I was supposed to want. And for that one moment with the Loretta Lynn and all these wonderful, awful folks, the thing that I should want most was the very thing I wanted. Just being here, just seeing them, just being here. To offer that bread and shine that light by just being here.

I had, at that one moment, the only rest I've ever found: to hear good news and just be here. Out here at the feast. Giving regard.

Right now, for at least this moment, I had a Crucified Heart. A shining wound. The right intention. To honor and uphold and welcome and just be here. The joy we offer, the joy in offering.

Offering this regard. This sign of His cross, my share in His joy. This sorrow and longing. This anguish and light. This place we meet.

The gospel has only made me weirder. And the strange signs of this good news have only gotten weirder: Uno cards, gel pens, coffee, folding tables, boom boxes.

WHAT IS A BOOM BOX? An outdated sound machine. But what is the boom box that has been offered to us? A song. A revelation. The announcement of what's true. A way to be together. An invitation to the table. The radiance of His feast. A song by which Christ gathers a people to Himself.

What is Uno? A bad game. A dumb game. A really dumb game I'm tired of playing. But what is the Uno offered to us? A song. A revelation. The announcement of what's true. A way to be together. An invitation to the table. The radiance of His feast.

What is a donut? A worthless piece of sugar bread. But what is the donut offered to us? A song. A revelation. The announcement of what's true. A way to be together. An invitation to the table. The radiance of His feast. A song by which Christ gathers a people to Himself.

The joy we offer, the joy in offering. To share in something, and see each other clearly. The Person this is all about. The One we share in when we share in something like this. A life in Christ that includes me seeing them, them seeing me.

Ordinary things are sacred things when they are given things. And sometimes that's all we have to reveal Christ with: with what's given and what's taken. These quiet signs of Christ to a world that has lost all words and doesn't trust ours. Sometimes it seems there's nothing past this. Nothing past the deep gladness of just being here. Nothing to reveal Christ with but what's given and what's taken away.

Regard, company, places of rest. Quiet signs to a world that has lost all words, that has no words for what's coming toward them and what's going on inside them.

Our place to start again: our invitation to the table, our word about this Word. Our sign this news is true.

Today this man called us to himself with a boom box and Loretta Lynn. He made a table for us in this place. This way to be together in this place of pride and lies, trouble and loss, chaos and disaster. A reason to look at one another, laugh with one another. He gave us something to do, a way to honor, uphold, welcome, and just be here. A good word about this Word. And I was changed by this sign, this sign this news was true.

I looked around and saw the look of those who've been changed, the Look of Those Transfigured. The look of those upheld. When ruined gods, frightened children, and complete strangers are cleansed and presented and become themselves again. Even for just a little while. The look of a bunch of honored guests.

Held together by the feast right now. Scripture, friendship. good news, Ordinary Hospitality. Trust in Christ, regard for others. A Simple Rhythm, the fiercest song.

My long journey toward just sitting here. Out on stoops and tables like this. With gel pens and bad coffee and boom boxes. My long journey toward just sitting here, being friends, hearing promises. Toward a Simple Rhythm, a Crucified Heart, a more Ordinary Hospitality. My long journey toward the fiercest song. A long journey toward the Look of Those Transfigured. Toward something else to want most. Toward the joy of wasted time.

To give regard and be given in His name, and given to His joy. And to see Him more clearly as we give a more Ordinary Hospitality.

2

A TABLE CALLED MERCY

Another word for His dying and rising, Christ's generous offer of Himself to us

THE WORK OF REGARD, COMPANY, AND PLACES OF REST. That's the work I do now. The incarnate funk of just being here as a part-time chaplain.

To give regard. And be given in His name, and given to His joy. And to see Him clearly as I offer a more Ordinary Hospitality.

But I didn't have this work until I had words, until I got these words back. Abused, neglected, and alienated, for years I had no words for all the things coming toward me and all the things going on inside me, no words for all I'd lost, all the trouble I was in, all the lies I'd been told.

When I got words back, I kept repeating them. The words that have held me together. The words I just won't stop repeating here.

The journey toward just sitting here, the journey toward this work, has been a journey toward those words, a journey toward the words I say again and again. A long journey toward getting a few good words back. A few good words about what this is all about, about the Person this is all about. A few good words for the few good things I still believed in, and the words that make up the heading of each chapter:

The Feast of Bread and Light. A Table Called Mercy. A Crucified Heart.

A Simple Rhythm. An Ordinary Hospitality. The Look of Those Transfigured.

This memoir will have this repetition. It's how I think and how I make my way through things. It has been my reassurance as I've written. When I find the right words, I use them, and I repeat them. I repeat them because these words are true, they are some of the few good things that are not lies. They are the few good words about the few good things I still believe in. I repeat those few words to hold onto those few things that are not lies.

I have only been held together by a few good words. A few good words about this Word, a little song about this feast.

The words I've said again and again are all I know to say and the only way I know to say it. And these few words are the way I've moved through pride and lies, trouble and loss, chaos and disaster. They are how I've found the table in this place. These are my words for the table in this place. This place where the worst can happen and nothing makes sense and everything falls apart. And the Person this is still all about.

I am a liturgical person. My life is a liturgy, rhythm, song, repetition. The liturgy, rhythm, and song my denomination gave me.

Liturgy, rhythm, and song are how I move through confusion and pain. Liturgy, rhythm, and song are how I can hurt and lose and feel and still be gentle. Liturgies, rhythms, and songs that deepen my trust, shepherd my attention, and give me back to others. They are how I have become a rescued, led, and given thing. Liturgy, rhythm, and song are my simple life with this good news. They are how I am cleansed and presented by this good news. Presented as this offering. And all through

His Spirit and all of it a mending. Good news coming to me in gentle, lapping waves. News that cannot change but continues to change us.

Word and song, word and song, word and song. I repeat the words that are my song. I repeat the words because it feels like singing. And singing feels like being held together. And singing always feels like just about the exact opposite of falling apart.

Singing feels like being cleansed and presented. And all through His Spirit, and all of it a mending.

And this is my song:

The Feast of Bread and Light. A Table Called Mercy. A Crucified Heart. A Simple Rhythm. A more Ordinary Hospitality. The Look of Those Transfigured.

When I had those words I had the intention I'd thought I'd lost, the intention to be given, to be a friend to the crushed, a part-time chaplain, to visit the people the worst has happened to, to offer those things by which Christ gathers them to Himself. The intention He gave back to me. The intention to be a chaplain. To be a good haunted house.

When I had those words I had my song: the fierce song of regard, company, and places of rest. The fierce song of gentleness, grief, and gladness.

It is hard to say exactly how this is, how the gentle lapping waves work, except that the words have become the way I live and the way I see. I only see as clearly as the words I have. And I can only live according to the words I have.

The Feast of Bread and Light. A Table Called Mercy. A Crucified Heart.

A Simple Rhythm. An Ordinary Hospitality. The Look of Those Transfigured.

AND WHY DID I NEED THEM, those few good words about those few good things that life was still about? Those words I keep repeating because of what life was like.

Because life was like a great ocean. And the ocean was all I'd lost and all the trouble I was, all the lies I'd been told, and the pride that had been my only shepherd. The ocean, this wild country, those five years.

This ocean, this wild country, this place of pride and lies, trouble and loss, chaos and disaster. A place without words. Where there were no such things as seen, safe, and fed. Where I was tremendously hurt, scared, and upset. Where I didn't even know what I was supposed to want, after I was abused, neglected, alienated.

In that ocean, great, percussive, overlapping waves called trouble and loss. In that ocean, a great undertow called pride and lies. In that ocean, a great sea monster called chaos and disaster. In that ocean we are flailing—ruined gods, frightened children, complete strangers. In that ocean there is only flailing. A flailing called pride, a flailing called our hardness of heart. A flailing called defending ourselves, taking things back, and making things right.

In that ocean everyone is flailing and everything is falling apart. That's what it seemed like to me. It didn't feel like there was anything life was about. Crushed, abandoned, alienated, I came to believe life was like that great ocean. A place where we get crushed by what life's like.

A place without words. Where there was no such thing as seen or safe or fed. Where I didn't even know what I was supposed to want. And where I only knew I wanted that deeper note of rest.

And it still feels like that. It feels like that because it is like that.

That is what life is like. But it is not what life is about. Because mercy is what life's about. And mercy is the table in this place. The Person this is all about.

The Feast of Bread and Light is set at a Table Called Mercy. The table set by His dying and rising. The table set by the gracious offer of Himself. The offer of Himself to helpless sinners.

The feast of who He is set at the table of what He's done.

What has He done? He has offered Himself to us on the hard wood of the cross.

What is this mercy? This mercy is cleansing, provision, and rest. The cleansing of pride and lies, provision for trouble and loss, rest from chaos and disaster. We sit at this table and keep this feast—helpless sinners, honored guests, humble servants.

At this table there is only stillness. The stillness of not taking things back or making things right. An undeserved stillness called rescued, led, given. The stillness of a Crucified Heart.

I believe this ocean is what life is like. And this table is what life's about. The Person this is all about. I believe that life is like getting crushed by these great overlapping, percussive waves. But I believe that life is about receiving mercy at this table. Life is like an ocean and life is about this table. Both are true and I don't know how.

We are in this ocean, and at that table. In this ocean, and at that table.

For years this has been my question. Is life an ocean or table? Table or ocean? Does the ocean swallow the table? Or will the table part the ocean?

Is there solid ground here? Is it mercy or disaster? Mercy or disaster? Mercy or disaster?

AT FIRST MY VOTE WAS DISASTER. I voted in favor of everything falling apart. Crushed by a mentor, abandoned by a denomination, alienated from a movement, left in an ocean. Crashing and burning on the idea of myself as a pastor. Left flailing, in a place without words, where there was no such thing as seen or safe or fed. Where I didn't even know what I was supposed to want. And where I only knew I wanted rest.

What do I mean by *trouble*? I mean all the things coming toward us. Things that are bigger than you, more than you can hold. You name it: accidents, afflictions, abuse, death.

What do I mean by *loss*? I mean all the things going on inside us.

When there's something coming toward you it awakens things inside you, and you are at the mercy of those things as well, at the mercy of tremendous things inside yourself. The most tremendous, most powerful thing going on inside us is loss. Loss means the most important things we need are gone.

Honor and regard are gone, and it hurts, and that loss is felt as shame. Assurance and strength are gone, and it's scary, and that loss is felt as fear. Meaning and purpose are gone, and it's upsetting, and that loss is felt as despair.

The loss of those things is so powerful because it's the loss of what we need to be okay. We have all those things coming toward us, and all those things going on inside us, and we are no match for either. Tossed around by both, at the mercy of all the things coming toward us and all the things going on inside us.

And then, beneath the great waves of trouble and loss, that great undertow of pride and lies.

What do I mean by *lies*? Those things that are not true. The wrong idea about what this is all about, a bad expectation of what life's about, and what matters. The greatest lie I know—the most fundamental—is that life is about us. Learning that we are important but not the point is the slow work of a lifetime.

What do I mean by *pride*? Pride is the trust we have in ourselves. The thing in us that says we can take things back and make things right. The thing in us that says we can win instead of lose. The thing in us that just starts flailing. A blindness, a compulsion we can't get rid of.

What do I mean by *disaster*? Ruin, collapse, dissolution, disintegration, crumbling, crisis, abyss, breakdown, rupture, shattering, things falling apart. That sinking, horrible feeling that we're not going to make it.

What do I mean by *chaos*? Incoherence, incomprehension, disorder, disorientation, disharmony, discontinuity. Bewilderment. When nothing makes sense. When everything is nonsense.

That's what happened when I was crushed, abandoned, alienated. I was in that wild country, and the wild country was an ocean. This place of pride and lies, trouble and loss, chaos and disaster. And mercy is what I found. Mercy is the table in this place. This place where the worst can happen and nothing makes sense and everything falls apart.

The Feast of Bread and Light. The feast of His own life. Set at the Table Called Mercy. The table set by the gracious offer of Himself. The table set by His dying and rising. A Table Called Mercy.

A Table Called Mercy. One of the words I had to get back.

A table for ruined gods, frightened children, complete strangers. A Christian is someone who sits at this table, partakes of this feast. A Christian is someone who hears this news, eats this bread, and sees this light, someone who has received mercy. This cleansing, provision, and rest. In this place of pride and lies, trouble and loss, chaos and disaster. Mercy is our table in this place.

After I'd been crushed, abandoned, alienated, my life was a mess and my mind was not my friend. My career did not exist. And I had just turned thirty. The dirty thirties, baby. That wild country, that great ocean called the early thirties.

Crushed, abandoned, alienated, and in a place without words, I started working for an ecumenical outreach organization. I started working as that part-time chaplain. The title was "street pastor" but that was not a title I understood. I worked with a church, but I didn't have a church. I couldn't be a pastor, not when I didn't have a church. Not when I had crashed and burned on the idea of myself as a pastor. Not when I didn't even know if I was supposed to be doing any of this anymore.

A pastor preaches and teaches, and I knew I wouldn't be doing either. I was supposed to offer presence. I was a chaplain. I just didn't know what all that word would mean.

I had to raise support to be a part-time chaplain. My other part-time job was as a caregiver. I was supposed to be a full-time pastor and now I was a part-time caregiver and a part-time chaplain.

When I started, they sent me to a missions conference. I had no idea what I was doing, and they wanted me to go to a missions conference.

It was at a retreat center in the mountains. It was full of lots of wonderful people who really loved Jesus. And I didn't want to meet them.

I sat in the back of the auditorium, all crushed and abandoned and alienated. Part-time evangelist, kinda sorta chaplain. And I had a vision in that auditorium.

You have to be careful when you say you've had a vision. You don't want to sound like one of those people who gets visions.

When I say I had a vision, I only mean I had a clear picture in my mind's eye.

A lot of things I saw in my mind's eye at the time only brought embarrassment and pain. Terrible things I wrote another book about. But this picture in my mind's eye brought a stillness to my heart and mind, as if all was settled.

The picture was blurry and dark at the edges, but at the center was a good kind of eerie light, a soft glow so that you could see a table. It was a vision of a table. Lit by a light that was odder, kinder, gentler, and better than light has ever been.

No one in the auditorium or at the missions conference had been talking about tables. Or singing about tables. I didn't know tables were going to be important. I didn't even know what the work I do now was even going to look like. I didn't know anything.

I had the Holy Spirit and I didn't know what to do. A friend of mine had said that. A stoop friend I'd made in the first few days.

But all of a sudden, in that auditorium, I had a vision of that friend of mine at a table—a clear picture of all of it. And I knew it was a Table Called Mercy. That mercy was the table in this ocean, in this wild country.

It was dark at the edges, and it was not a fancy table, and it was not a fancy friend. It was an ordinary wooden table except that it made me cry to see he was there. That clear picture of a friend of mine. An ordinary friend.

A table with an odder, kinder, gentler, brighter light, that felt like an invitation into the very heart of things. An ordinary thing that struck a deeper note than ordinary things, that struck that deeper note of rest. There was a table at the very heart of things. At the very heart of all we've lost, all the trouble we're in, all the lies we'd been told. It was a Table Called Mercy. And my friend was there.

The Feast of Bread and Light was set at the Table Called Mercy. There was a friend of mine at a Table Called Mercy. And the table was cleansing, provision, rest. A feast that changes what we want.

This was a friend I'd made already. My friend, a younger looking, long-haired Mister Rogers. My friend, a thin man in his late forties with a gentle smile, a sense of humor, and acute schizophrenia.

An ocean of pride and lies, trouble and loss, chaos and disaster. This place without words, where there was no such thing as seen or safe or fed. Where I didn't even know what I was supposed to want. And where I only wanted rest. A hot mess. A part-time chaplain barely hanging in there at a missions conference.

And then a vision in an auditorium. And knowing it was mercy. That mercy was the table in this place. This place for us to be. This way for us to be together. This place we meet.

Knowing it is mercy that makes Him known. That mercy sets the feast. This place for us to be. This way for us to be together.

Being there, getting to be there, seemed to be what life was about. Being there, getting to be there, was point. To honor, uphold, and welcome, and just be there. To offer bread and hold out light by just being there.

The simple goodness of just being there. The simple goodness of it. This way to be together. This place we were supposed to be. An honored guest at the very heart of things. This brighter light. This cleansing, provision, and rest. This place we meet.

Outside of special visions, my friend and I are still together often. On Fridays when we make our place of rest, on Sunday when we do church.

But that was the first time I guess I really saw him. Saw him front and center like that. He and the table lit by a soft, eerie light. A good kind of eerie light.

My friend lives in a care home down the street from our church and is allowed to walk around and do what everyone else does as long as he comes back for his pills and doesn't leave town. He's at all the little things we do.

I should tell you what he's like.

My friend, a younger looking, long-haired Mister Rogers. My friend, a thin man in his late forties with a gentle smile, a sense of humor, and acute schizophrenia.

Sometimes my friend looks at you like he just thought of something good and can't wait to tell you. When he looks at you that way he smiles.

It's his smile that gets to you. His smile is his joy and mischief, his intelligence and surprise and politeness all at once. That smile makes his eyes bend at the corners. It's a smile that does something to you. It turns bad days to good days. You are changed by this strange man who smiled at you. The fact that you're there and he's there and you're there together. That bright gentleness, his odd gladness.

You are changed by that gladness so that you are glad too. You smile. You are changed by this man you're looking at, this man looking back at you. The smile is his gladness.

It's his smile that bends the corners of his eyes, but it's his eyes—his startling, clear eyes—that are his grief, that carry the sadness of his life. Sometimes those eyes look at you with a grief best left unsaid, like something has just happened in his mind's eye—whether memory or premonition, you cannot tell—and there is no word for it; only the sad look on his face. And you are touched by that look, too. Those eyes are his sorrow. That bright gentleness, his odd gladness. And all the sudden grief.

His smile and those sad eyes can make you someone else. You begin to feel your own life more. You are changed by the smile and sad eyes of an adult male with acute schizophrenia. Honored guest at a table. The sorrow and gladness of a friend of yours.

You seeing him, him seeing you. Changed by the time you've shared. Changed by the Person this is all about. Changed by the joy we offer, the joy in offering. What's given and what's taken. This place we're supposed to be. This way to be together. The One we share in whenever we share something.

This brighter light. This cleansing, provision, and rest. This place we're supposed to be. This place we meet.

He'll stop me and talk wherever I am. Those moments of sadness or laughter, those moments when he talks and I stop to listen, those moments when we're together, all this wasted time, these places for us to be, are like a mirror in which he almost catches a glimpse of himself—almost gets a good look at his own face, and almost understands who he is.

He tells me how the schizophrenia had made him a stranger to himself. His brain goes fuzzy; nothing makes sense anymore. A wave crashes in and he is not there anymore. All is chaos. Everything is nonsense. He touches his head, shrugs his shoulders. This affliction swallows him. A shrieking fog. A shrieking fog so he cannot be sad or smile, so he cannot find his grief and gladness. Or that odd gentleness.

The smile and sadness suddenly disappear. The sorrow and gladness are gone and there's just this restlessness. A stunning incomprehension, an ugly incoherence. Angst and turmoil. He walks around with that stunning incomprehension, that ugly incoherence, and there is no way he'll stay very long. He shakes his head, agitated, like he is never where he's supposed to be, like things are never what they're supposed to be.

An ocean all around us. Where we get crushed by what life's like. When everyone's flailing and everything's falling apart. In a place without words. Where we're no match for what's coming toward us and what's going on inside us. Where there's no such thing as seen or safe or fed.

When he's walking around and shaking his head I know he is trying to hold on to himself. There's an ocean all around him and he's just flailing. This place of incoherence and pain. Just trying to be okay. Just trying to take things back, make things right. He's lost too much to be himself again.

My friend, a younger looking, long-haired Mister Rogers. My friend, a thin man in his late forties with a gentle smile, a sense of humor, and acute schizophrenia.

I see it in his face—what we can suddenly become in the incoherence and pain. I see it in all our faces. Some ruined god, some frightened child, some complete stranger.

The agitation, the restlessness, shaking his head and wandering around. Trying to make things right. My friend. My crushed friend. My friend crushed by this affliction.

I cannot explain it: that smile, that sadness, that restlessness, except to say he has been crushed. Crushed, swallowed, devoured by what life is like. Riven by incoherence and pain. No match for it. Tossed around by what's coming toward him and what's going on inside him. My crushed friend who is still glad.

THAT IS MY FRIEND. And what I had at the missions conference was a clear picture of that friend of mine at a table, and the two of us seeing each other. The two of us visiting. Wasting time. I saw him there, turning toward me, smiling, still a little sad. But not at all restless, not even a little confused. His gentleness, grief, and gladness. An odder, kinder, gentler light putting its glow on his face so I could clearly see it. A good, solemn look. A good, solemn look that said he knew what life's about, and he was where he was supposed to be. That he was himself again.

Seeing him like that made me feel like myself again.

This picture, dark at the edges, an odder, kinder, gentler light at the center so I could see him and I could see where he was. That he was at a table. This way to be together. This place we're supposed to be. And the One we share in when we share in something.

There was nothing special about that wooden table and nothing special about seeing him there, except that I was crying. It was an ordinary thing, except that I cried to see it. An ordinary thing that struck that deeper note of rest. The simple goodness of it. The simple goodness when there's finally something this is all about. The simple goodness of just being here. Finally where he was supposed to be. Honored guest at the very heart of things. This brighter light. This cleansing, provision, and rest. This place we meet.

And he was finally himself again, himself again forever. His honor restored, strength upheld, despair overturned. He would never be hurt, scared, upset. You could see it on his face, that there was no such thing as shame, fear, despair. His was the Look of

Those Transfigured. The look of those upheld. Cleansed and presented by this good news. Cleansed, presented, and himself again.

And I thought about who he was, and who I was. Who we were.

We are not the bread and we are not the light. And we are not the table and we are not the feast. But we are those who sit. And we are those who eat and we are those we see. And we are those who have been changed. And who we really are is who we are at this table. At this table by this good news.

We have the Look of Those Transfigured. The look of those changed by this feast. The feast set by His mercy.

I believe in that table. This Word to us. The feast of who He is sets the table of what He's done. And I believe in the Look of Those Transfigured. The look of those upheld. This brighter light. This cleansing, provision, rest. This place we meet.

A table in this ocean of pride and lies, trouble and loss, chaos and disaster. A little table in this great ocean.

LIFE IS FULL OF PRIDE AND LIES, trouble and loss, chaos and disaster. But I believe in their joyful end. A final gladness. A feast to change us. A table to give us back to God, ourselves, each other. I believe we are in this ocean, and at that table.

Our deepest longing—to be given back. Given back to God, ourselves, each other. To be at the table, the homecoming only offered in Him. Our deepest longing, this cleansing, provision, and rest. A life at this table.

And when I saw my friend transfigured, I knew the Lord wanted the crushed at His table. The Lord wanted the crushed at His table so they could be changed. There was a table at the very heart of all we've lost, all the trouble we're in, and all the lies we've been told. And this table is what life's about. The table is called mercy. And it is for the people the worst has happened to, the people who've been crushed by what life's like.

I had no idea what I was doing. But I had had a vision. And I at least knew that: *He wants the crushed at His table.*

I knew that my longing for Christ was the longing to see my crushed friend changed, to see that he had been given back to God, given back to himself. For him to have the Sabbath rest offered only in Christ. For him to be at that homecoming. To see him like that would make me feel like myself again. He would know what life's about, and I would know what life's about. Because Jesus was what life's about.

And joy was the Person this was all about. My longing for Christ was a longing to see the crushed upheld by this cleansing, provision, and rest. All the forgotten folks. To not be hurt, scared, and upset. Their honor restored, their strength upheld, their despair overturned by Christ.

I had a spark of joy again. It's color blue, its light bright. That deeper note of rest. And joy was the longing to see the crushed upheld. Christ was the joy, and His joy was to have His people back, because they know where they're supposed to be. They know there is a table to uphold the crushed.

It was a fierce longing. It still is. Those who sit at this table are fed with that fierce longing. The fierce longing for Christ to be revealed to wounded, selfish people. A longing for this news to be true. A longing for a more Ordinary Hospitality.

I had that vision, felt that longing, and heard these words in my heart: "Will you serve my table?"

I was a mess and I heard it anyway.

"Will you serve my table?"

That was what I had to go on: a vision, a longing, a question.

AND SO THE FIRST WORD I got back was *mercy*. The feast set by mercy. That mercy, I knew, was God's steadfast love, His involvement, His making things right. His dying and rising. The gracious offer of Himself. A gift offered to us by His death, vindicated by His rising, fulfilled by His coming.

And Christians are people who sit at this table, partake of this feast. A people mended by His dying and rising. Cleansed and presented all at once by His dying and rising.

A Table Called Mercy. One of the words I had in this place.

I knew it was a table for the crushed, but I didn't know how to serve that table. I had to get those other words back. To get those few words in this wild country. To get those words before

I made my way to sad Grandma's house, before I sat here on this stoop.

My journey to the fiercest song. A journey toward wasted time. A journey toward just sitting here. Toward that brighter light, that darker shade of blue, that deeper note of rest.

A journey toward these other words: *A Simple Rhythm. A Crucified Heart. An Ordinary Hospitality. The Look of Those Transfigured.*

I've said the words before, and I'll say the words again. And I'll say a little more about them now.

I BELIEVE IN THE FEAST OF BREAD AND LIGHT. I believe in a Table Called Mercy.

And I believe in a Simple Rhythm of Scripture, prayer, and service.

That Simple Rhythm. One of the words I had to get back. One of the few good words about the feast right now, the table in this place. The Person this is all about. One of the few good things that are not lies.

The good news is our means of grace: the gospel working through His Spirit in the building of His fellowship.

A Simple Rhythm is life with this good news. Good news that rescues our trust in Him, shepherds our attention toward Him, and gives us to one another in His name. This happens by the power of the Spirit, the One who makes it possible to believe in the gospel and somehow live as if it were true. The One who leads us from hearing through prayer toward offering.

I sit at this table and keep this feast as I take hold of this Simple Rhythm, so that each day I am rescued by the gospel and die with Him, led through His Spirit and rise with Him, and am given to His fellowship and share in the joy of His return.

But the strangest thing is the last thing: His return is the amen to His death and resurrection, and His fellowship is the amen of His gospel. The amen of His gospel is having His people back.

If you've been crushed, abandoned, and alienated from God's people, that is the last thing you want to believe. At that point the last thing you trust is other people, simply because no matter how much you love them, you cannot trust them to not be horrible. And if people are horrible and if you cannot trust them, you do not want to be where they are and you do not want to serve them.

But that is the thing: other people are the inevitability of good news. Good news gathers a wounded, lovely, selfish people.

And this is hard. You simply cannot believe that other people are at the feast. You cannot believe other wounded, selfish people could be associated with this cleansing, provision, and rest. How can the feast be safe when people are just awful? When you love them and cannot trust them not to be horrible? When you simply cannot believe that you are going to have to learn how to be with people again? The nonsense of that kind of longing and sorrow. The nonsense of that kind of anguish and light. The nonsense of it all being called joy.

The hardest thing to count on, then, is the amen of the gospel. And if you're like me and you love people but don't trust them, how do you count on the amen of the gospel?

But it can't be helped. By His steadfast love, His making things right, His dying, rising, and coming, Jesus rescues and prepares a people for Himself. I believe that. I'm sitting here typing this sentence and I believe that.

I believe that, but after being crushed, abandoned, and alienated, church is also the last thing I want to do, or be a part of, or ever make myself vulnerable to ever again. Because if there's one thing I believe it's that God's people are sacred to Him and must be treated well, and if there's another thing I believe it's that God's people are unacceptable and will devour you completely. I believe God's people are sacred and unacceptable. And that this is all nonsense.

How do you become a part of something that you love but cannot trust? When you don't really know if you believe that when we get together we become a better thing?

Perhaps my only trust is this: that good news gathers a people who can be changed. That we can all be changed by who He is and what He's done. That it is inevitable that we will all be changed. That we will all be cleansed and presented.

Cleansed as helpless sinners. Mended as honored guests. Presented as humble servants. All at once by His dying and rising. Day by day as we hear this news and offer a more Ordinary Hospitality.

We've been asked to serve the inevitability of His people—the bitter feast. The bitter feast is Christ as well. It is whenever wounded, selfish people are given to wounded, selfish people.

I BELIEVE IN THE FEAST OF BREAD OF LIGHT. I believe in a Table Called Mercy.

I believe in a Simple Rhythm. And I believe in a *Crucified Heart.*

One of those words I had to get back. One of those few good words about the table in this place. One of the few good words about the feast right now. One of the few good things that are not lies.

By a Crucified Heart I only mean that those who sit at this table, keep this feast, and hear this news now have an inheritance. The inheritance of those who have received mercy is a new heart—what I call a Crucified Heart. If wounded, selfish people can sit at the table and be changed, the change is a Crucified Heart.

A Crucified Heart. A stillness called faith, hope, and love. A stillness of being rescued, led, given. The stillness where we don't take things back or make things right. The stillness of those who hear, pray, and offer.

A Crucified Heart means that ruined gods, frightened children, and complete strangers can sit at a table and be changed. Cleansed as helpless sinners. Mended as honored guests.

Presented as humble servants. And the change is called faith, hope, and love.

A Crucified Heart, then, is a heart that now knows God and trusts in Christ instead of pride and lies. A heart that trusts Christ with trouble and loss. A heart that entrusts itself to others in the midst of chaos and disaster. A heart that entrusts itself to others for the sake of their trust in Christ.

It's what happens to those who sit at this table, keep this feast, and hear this news. The feast that changes what we trust, pay attention to, even want, so that we trust in Christ instead of pride and lies. So that we trust Christ with trouble and loss. So that we entrust ourselves to others for the sake of their trust in Him.

The trust He rescues called faith. The attention He leads called hope. The gift of ourselves called love.

A Crucified Heart is what happens when there's nothing left to do, nothing left but share in who He is and what He's done. When there's nothing left but the people who are at this table. Nothing left but the offer of bread and the shining of light. Nothing left but rest. Nothing left but to deepen that trust in Him. Nothing left but to get a more Crucified Heart.

Was it possible to live in this ocean? This place of pride and lies, trouble and loss, chaos and disaster? Only by an undeserved stillness. Only if I could be rescued, led, given. Only if I could sit at this table, keep this feast, hear this news. Only if I could be changed. Only if I could find that stillness at that table.

Only if I could be changed in such a way that I became even more myself. Only if my friend and I can be changed in such a way that we become even more like ourselves. And only if all of it could be called rest.

Only if I could catch a glimpse of myself already at this table, already at the feast. A glimpse of myself already changed.

My friend sees me riding my bike on a cold day. I stop what I'm doing, and he stops what he's doing. This long-haired Mister Rogers.

What did I feel on that day? That the work of a part-time evangelist and kinda sorta chaplain was too difficult. That it was all too stupid and too hard.

"John," he says. He takes my hand in his.

"John," he says, "Your hands are cold."

"We need to get you some gloves," he says. That sadness, that smile. "Your hands are cold."

That sadness in his eyes, that smile in his mouth. This way to be together. To share in something, and see each other clearly. The Person this is all about.

And then his closeness. He puts his hand on my head. A hand on my head that is his gentleness. His hand on my head and a quick gassy laugh and I am changed, knowing that this is all about the honored guest at the very heart of things.

Sometimes if you've had some food and he has a napkin he'll lean over and wipe your face real gently. Sometimes if he sees you getting in the car he'll close the door behind you so softly you feel like a baby in a blanket.

Moments like that. A clearing, an opening, a bit of light. Some note that's struck, some strange sign of the table in this place, some song about this feast. Some regard, some tender, basic, visible sign of the reality of Christ, the forgiveness of sins, and the homecoming offered in Him.

Another day he's helping me paint a wall. We stop and have some pizza, and he looks at me, his eyes clear and wet. He touches his head.

"You make the bad spirits go away," he says. And I knew it wasn't me, it was the moment we were in. In that moment, with pizza and something to do together, a clearing, a table, some bit of light, some small sign of the Sabbath rest offered in Christ. I knew he was right and he was wrong. That it was and wasn't me.

Just two men who know where they're supposed to be. The Person this is all about. Just two men singing to each other. Just two men telling each other something beautiful, letting each other know that nothing that happens gets to change what life's about. Just two men at a table.

During Covid, our ministry stood outside and held out coffee on winter days. My friend would walk by, and I would say his name from across the street. He would hear his name and find me there. He would take the coffee and we would look at each other. His eyes both clear and misty. Eyes somehow both cloudy and righteous.

And we are both somehow changed by the moment we're in, changed by giving and receiving, what's given and what's taken, me seeing him, him seeing me. The light is when Christ gave Himself; the light is when we go and see each other.

A life in Christ that includes giving coffee to our sad and tired friends, for the simple radiance of it. Just two men singing to each other, telling each other something beautiful. Two men singing to each other in this place. Telling each other this news is true.

I look back and perhaps that is what I wanted to know—that there is a way to not be annihilated by pride and lies, by trouble and loss, chaos and disaster. Not be disintegrated by great, overlapping, percussive waves. That the self could be upheld in the face of such obliterating forces. That I was still there under all the rubble of what happened to me.

That is what the Crucified Heart is: the self upheld by this good news. In the face all the things coming toward us and all the things going on inside: upheld by this good news, and by those few small signs that this news is true.

Good news and a more Ordinary Hospitality putting me back together, putting this flailing thing back together, this scarecrow thing called myself, all riven and torn by pride and lies, trouble and loss, ruin and disaster.

This Crucified Heart. The great pain of it. The stillness of not taking things back and not making thing right. The stillness of hearing, praying, and offering.

A Crucified Heart is how we meet our own wounded soul. The stillness of not taking things back and not making things right is how we finally *realize* we're hurt, scared, and upset. A Crucified Heart is how we meet our own wounded soul—its shame, fear, and despair, its loss of honor, strength, purpose. Chances are we have not felt the screaming loss of things because pride and lies have protected us from it.

And so now the question is: Can we trust Christ with the screaming loss of things? So that we can finally be given, instead of just flailing?

And the answer is: Only a Crucified Heart can be given. Only a Crucified Heart can trust Christ with the screaming loss of things. And only good news crucifies the heart. This light by which we see Him, this bread by which He gives us to Himself.

Cleansed and presented by this good news. Presented as an offering. And all through His Spirit and all of it a mending.

With a Crucified Heart, our pain becomes sorrow, our sorrow becomes longing, our longing that becomes joy. This brighter light, this darker shade of blue. This fierce song of gentleness, this grief, this gladness.

I BELIEVE IN THE FEAST OF BREAD AND LIGHT. I believe in a Table Called Mercy.

I believe a Simple Rhythm. I believe in a Crucified Heart. I believe in those words.

And I believe in a more *Ordinary Hospitality*, this ministry of presence. The strangest sign, the fiercest song.

One of the words I had to get back. One of those few good words about the table in this place. One of the few good words about the Person this is all about. One of the few good things that are not lies.

Our service. Our announcement. Our word about this Word. Our invitation to His table. The song by which Christ gathers the crushed to Himself. Our sign that this news is true.

Those who sit at that table and keep that feast offer a more Ordinary Hospitality.

When I had been crushed, abandoned, and alienated, when I had crashed and burned on an idea of myself, there seemed to be so little I believed in and so little I could work with. So much of what I thought was my inheritance in Christ was gone. There was only, it seemed, a few haggard realities left. No career or grand vision. Only a few good things that were not lies. Just a few shambling, decomposing signs of Him.

All there was to do was to take hold of a Simple Rhythm, get a more Crucified Heart, give a more Ordinary Hospitality. The only rest I'd find was hearing good news and just being here. The feast right now. The table in this place.

That was all I had. This Ordinary Hospitality: the regard I could give, the company I could keep, the places of rest I could make. A sign that this news was true. This meager revelation of Christ to the wounded soul and the hardened heart.

I wish Ordinary Hospitality could be something other than just being here. But it mostly isn't.

My friend—the handsome, long-haired Mister Rogers—can't really hold a conversation. More than thirty seconds and he's lost. A lot of words confuse him. He can't focus at a Bible study. He doesn't follow the things you explain.

He's someone you wait for. Waiting for him to say what he needs to say, and only if he wants to say it.

We played Uno once. Was the radiance of Christ there? Was it a sign that this news is true? I don't know.

The next time I asked him to play Uno he looked at me, and then looked down at the steam floating from his coffee. He shook his head.

"I'm trying to focus on my cup of coffee."

No sustained conversation. No games. No Bible study. But he likes to have you sit with him, and look at him, and just say something every now and then. All this wasted time. To honor, uphold, and just be here. The light of Christ pouring through the stained-glass window of wasted time.

I was supposed to serve that table. But serving that table was going to be about learning to be with my friend. The deep gladness of just being there with my friend, who didn't want to talk, who didn't want to speak, but who enjoyed having you sit there. Sitting here, being friends, hearing promises.

The ministry of presence was all I had to reveal Christ to my friend. This quiet sign to a crushed friend. It felt like the only light I could hold out to his scattered mind was the light of Christ pouring through the stained-glass window of wasted time.

A light held out to the crushed. My announcement to my adult friend with acute schizophrenia.

I STEP OUT OF MY TRUCK IN THE HEAT. Another friend gets in and I take him somewhere. We stop for him to get groceries. I think, what is this? So many rides, so many coffees, so much small talk, so much time spent just listening. So much time wasted—unless there is no such thing as wasted time. Unless this is the only time that wasn't wasted. Unless this is an offering. Unless it is radiance, the light of Christ poured in through the stained-glass window of wasted time.

Stupid and useless, unless these small offerings are an invitation to His table. Unless this is a song. Unless this really is some strange sign this news is true.

When I'm doing these things I have to imagine myself singing over the wounded, lovely, selfish people. When I'm visiting, walking, sitting, listening, giving regard, coming alongside, I'm singing a song. I'm saying, by these few things, that nothing that happen gets to change what life's about.

I sing about Him until He gets here. Learning His gentleness, entering His grief, sharing His gladness. Learning how to be with people again. Serving the inevitability of His people, the inevitability of this good news.

My craft, my trade, is learning how to be with people. Learning to be a friend to the crushed. To be cleansed and presented. To become the gracious offer of myself to the world as it is, people as they are, the moments that we're in, and the situation as it stands. Learning how to be good company in this place where the worst happens and nothing makes sense and everything falls apart.

That is all there is. The feast for now. The table in this place. Those few good things that are not lies. The only trick is learning to call it enough.

I refer to regard, company, and places of rest as "offerings" because they have to be. They have to be an offering or they are not given in His name. If they are not an offering, they are a betrayal of His gentleness, grief, and gladness. A betrayal of His name and His joy, and they do not announce the Person this is all about.

They must stay offerings. They must be left in the world as offerings, announcements, and signs, not as opportunities or coercion or a way to enlist people into something else. And certainly never ever ever as something by which to fix them. They must remain what they are: a word about a Word, a song about a feast. A gentleness, a grief, a gladness. A revelation. The fierce longing for Christ to be revealed the wounded soul and the hardened heart.

When these offerings become something else, they become something worse.

If a more Ordinary Hospitality is only possible because good news crucifies heart, then these offerings have their own integrity and do their own work. We can leave these things in the world as they are. They are holy unto themselves and they don't have to do anything else. They cast their own light; they are their own song. The goodness of them is goodness for its own sake.

The announcement must be left alone. It must be left there as an announcement. All these quiet signs of Him must be left at that. Left out there in this place of pride and lies, trouble and loss, chaos and disaster.

It seems to me that we offer a lot of things in hopes of a certain outcome. The most common outcome is people getting better. But we have not been asked to control outcomes, or manage results. We have only been asked to offer ourselves to the world as it is, to people as they are, to the moments we're in, to the situation as it stands.

We have to lose our trust in what happens so that our trust can be in what we offer. We have to let go of outcomes so we can be cleansed by this news, presented as this offering. To be confident only in what we offer, so that Christ might be revealed.

We begin to trust that what we offer is more solid and real than what might happen. This offering, this song, is more real than the apparition or premonition of disaster. It is more real than trouble and loss, because it is a sign that this news is true. The announcement is more real than the possibility of trouble. The invitation is more real than the likelihood of failure.

It is enough for any ministry to simply be a sign of the Person this is all about. It is enough for any ministry to do it only for the goodness of the thing itself, for who it reveals and whose light it casts. For it to be only the radiance of the preached Word and the Lord's Supper. For us to do it only because of who Jesus is, and for the sake of their return to Him.

Offered to a world that has lost more than it can possibly bear without some sign of the Sabbath rest offered in Christ, to folks who have no words for all the things they've lost and all the trouble they're in and all the lies they've been told, and who don't trust our own words yet.

The ministry of presence is the impossible possibility. You and I are not ready for His joy, or for His gladness. We are only headed toward it.

On a long journey toward His joy. On a long journey toward His gladness.

I BELIEVE IN THE TABLE CALLED MERCY. I believe in a Simple Rhythm. I believe in a Crucified Heart. I believe in an Ordinary Hospitality. And I believe in the *Look of Those Transfigured*. One of those few good words about the table in this place. One of thew few good words about the Person this is all about. One of the few good things that are not lies.

I had been crushed by a mentor, abandoned by a denomination, and alienated from a movement. I had been left with all I'd lost, all the trouble I was in, all the lies I'd been told, with pride my only shepherd.

Left in an ocean of chaos and hard feelings, and finding only these few words. I spent a half decade finding these few good words, and finding out if I meant them.

Because I believe in these things, I find myself believing in one other thing—the Look of Those Transfigured. The look of those upheld. The fact that we can all be changed.

The Look of Those Transfigured: the look of gentleness, grief, and gladness, the glory of their sad, tired faces.

I SIT AT A BONFIRE IN THE BACKYARD of a few dear friends of ours. As things get going, my friend's wife asks me to pray. I know the intent was merely to honor me. She asks me to pray and I say, "You can ask anyone to pray, I'm not a real pastor." And I flinch at the sharpness in my own voice.

What was that sharpness? That sharpness was my grief. The wounded honor of a ruined god. The sharpness was the sudden pang of grief I'd felt over what my life wasn't. The way I'd crashed and burned on an idea of myself as a pastor. The loss of who I thought I was and what I thought life was going to be like. The sharp and sudden grief of being a complete nobody.

We had moved to this town years ago with the understanding that I was to become a pastor. But then a lot of things happened. My mind turned on me (another book), a mentor crushed me, an institution left me, a movement went the wrong way.

I felt a sting, the sting of being a nobody instead of a somebody. The sting of a would-be pastor, now a part-time evangelist and kinda sorta chaplain. How I wasn't a real pastor, how I had been disqualified by a bad boss and a broken mind. How I was this instead: a weird walking third space. A chaplain who only offers presence. A big lanky lumbering crusty decrepit decomposing sign of the reality of Christ, the forgiveness of sins, and the homecoming offered only in Him.

The people gathered around the bonfire were people I'd spent a lot of time with—a lot of coffee, a lot of rides in cars, a lot of time hearing. And it felt like that's all I offered. Time. Wasted time.

All I had to show for it, for all the years my wife and I spent in this town, was this loose affiliation, this loose network of bonfires, crafts tables, open mics, spiritual retreats. This ministry of presence. These few small quiet sign of Him. These few words about this Word.

All I had to show for it was bonfires like this. All I had to show for it was a Simple Rhythm, a Crucified Heart, a more Ordinary Hospitality.

The means of grace, an undeserved stillness, and a few places we were supposed to be. A confederacy of third spaces. Little shambly, cozy spaces where no one got devoured. A word or two about this Word. These few small signs of Him. A few fragile sanctuaries in the land of sin and death. These fragile third spaces, these gentler ways to be together, the fruit of the regard we'd given and the company we'd kept.

A place to be when there is nowhere to be. A few places of rest. That's what I had to show for it. A few invitations to His table, a few words about that Word, a few songs about a feast.

BEFORE I'D GOTTEN MYSELF all crushed, abandoned, and alienated, I'd wanted to be the faithful pastor of a small church. I'd wanted to be with people I loved and belong to something I could count on. I'd wanted to be a part of something bigger than myself. I wanted to be an ordained pastor of a solid denomination.

And when I was asked to pray at the bonfire, I realized I was not. I was a part-time evangelist and kinda sorta chaplain who helped start a couple of third spaces.

And I was hurt. It hurt to not be a pastor. I loved Scripture and I loved people and it hurt to not be a pastor. But there was no excuse for my tone, and no reason for hostility.

I made apologies to the wife of my dear friend, who was gracious. Afterward I took two honored guests at our bonfire home, two friends who stay at a care home downtown. A man and woman in their late twenties/early thirties. They can both be very quiet, very cryptic, very closed.

Those spaces can be hard for them. They like to keep to themselves, but they also like to come. I've spent years with them now, and they come because they know me and because it's something to do and somewhere to be. The woman usually has curt replies. She has a hard time with even a simple greeting. Every question she takes as an accusation, every compliment as a slight, every encouraging word as a threat. She recoils somehow, she gets defensive, caustic, almost hostile.

I'm reminded she is one of the people the worst has happened to.

I'm reminded that all she really has is nothing at all. I'm reminded that when you have nothing then all you have left is your refusal. Your refusal any question. Your refusal of any compliment. The only honor left is to be alien to all of it.

What do I see in her replies? I see her repulsion, the unconquerable loathing of the utter stranger. Stranger to me, to this moment, to what I'm asking.

I left the bonfire. I drove them home. They got ready to get out of the car. I said, "It was a joy to have y'all there."

She said, "It was a joy to be there." Her face softening, her eyes gently pointed at me. The Look of Those Transfigured. The look of those upheld. When ruined gods, frightened children, and utter strangers are cleansed and presented and become themselves again.

It was, I think, the first time she had said anything like that to me ever.

That's what I had. Instead of a church, I had moments like that.

In that moment, a clearing. Some brighter light. Some darker shade of blue.

Would I do it all again? Come here? Be here? Do this? Be a nobody instead of a somebody? Would I be crushed, abandoned, and alienated all over again for moments like this?

A part-time evangelist for moments like this? I knew I would do it all again.

I would do it all for the Look of Those Transfigured. To see the crushed upheld.

I would do it all again for the goodness of it, the deep gladness of it. I would do it all again to see people changed. I would do it all again to see Him more clearly. To learn His gentleness, enter His grief, and share His gladness.

I turned back to see the look I'd already heard in the tone of her voice, to see the Look of Those Transfigured. That thing she said as they got out of the car mattered more to me than a church or a career. It meant I had been given, and it meant I could be given by Christ to others. It meant Christ had been revealed somehow. Christ had given me others. And Christ had given me back to myself.

This stench, this color, this light. This deeper note of rest.

I had been on a long journey in a wild country. A long journey toward that look on her face. A long journey toward that gladness. A life journey toward being given. A million miles to wind up sitting here.

That moment struck that clear note of joy. There was in that note more joy than a million years of taking things back and making things right. Being there, getting to be there, seemed to be what life was about. The goodness of the thing itself.

A sign of the final gladness, the announcement of the joyful end of pride, lies, trouble, loss, chaos, and disaster.

This is all I had. These few moments, these few places for people to be.

Would I do it again? It was too late to ask. These people, these spaces, were my joy. This ministry was my joy. And joy was the only thing that would ever be enough. The Look of Those Transfigured.

To give regard, and be given in His name, and given to His joy. To see Him more clearly as we give a more Ordinary Hospitality. As we have bonfires. And give rides.

And what does joy do? It is simple. Joy upholds. Joy is the feast that holds us together.

I'D FELT THAT CLEAR NOTE of joy before and seen the look of those upheld. Up and down the gloomy, jagged edges of thirty-five years of life.

That deeper note of rest sounding clearer, shining brighter for the moments having become memories. Somehow having more radiance and being even more real for having become the distant past.

How had I forgotten? How had I forgotten this deep gladness?

Things like this:

Years ago, sitting in a lifeguard stand while a special needs camp used our facility. Seeing them from a distance: a parade, a train. People with every kind of disability, with college kids as their counselors, moving through the wilderness of camp, coming to swim here.

I was just out of college, cynical, depressed. And I remember seeing that procession of special needs folks, and I remember not wanting to miss it, just not wanting to miss out on this gladness. I remembered this procession was the most beautiful thing I'd ever seen. I felt that that I only wanted to join that procession. Felt myself say to a Lord I hardly believed in that I didn't want to miss it. I didn't want to miss out on what it's all about. The Person it's all about. That clear note of joy. A life in Christ that includes me seeing them, them seeing me. Honored guest at the very heart of things.

All this pride, lies, trouble, loss. Chaos and disaster. Then, suddenly: mercy anywhere, mercy anyway. Joy anywhere, joy anyway. Cleansing, provision, and rest. A table in this place.

And things like this:

My dad getting up out of his chair to hug me after an argument we had, soaring over his broken hips, hobbling to me with all his gentleness, grief, and gladness. Getting to be there seemed to be what life was about. Pierced by a reality that could only have the name of Jesus. That clear note of joy. That gentleness, grief, and gladness. Honored guest at the very heart of things.

And things like this:

Driving an hour into town to see a man, and only to hear him complain and be there while he got his bandage changed by a weary nurse while an infomercial played in the background. Seeing him there, not knowing what to say, but knowing it was better to be there and not know what to say than to know what to say and not be there. Just to say hello, just to be with him. For some reason pierced again by a reality that could only have the name of Jesus. Being there, getting to be there, seemed to be what life was about. That clear note of joy. That gentleness, grief, and gladness. The look of those upheld. Honored guest at the very heart of things.

And things like this:

Standing in a psych ward surrounded by the residents who I now call friends, friends who just want to see and be seen. Knowing it is so hard and awful that they're there, that they have to be there, but now that they're here together it is a joy. A gentleness, grief, and gladness. They gather slowly. The one who says, "You just came to see us, didn't you?" And I say, "Yes." And I mean it. And I find all my good reasons for giving up church pierced by a reality that could only have the name of Jesus. Being there, getting to be there, seemed to be what life was about. That clear note of joy. That gentleness, grief, and gladness. The joy we offer, the joy in offering. The Person this is all about.

The regard that was given, the company that was kept, and the places of rest we make, all strike, I hope, that clear note of joy. And I hope, and continue to hope, that there is more of life and what life's about in that one clear note of joy than in a million years of taking things back and making things right.

What is there for sinners and guests to learn except that only joy will do? That just as His dying and His rising will become His coming again, just as His gospel and Spirit become His fellowship, just as faith and hope become love, just as regard becomes company and places of rest, so His gentleness and grief become His gladness. His forgiveness and His company have nowhere to take us, nothing to become, but joy. The joy of return.

What sinners and guests are learning is that only His joy will do. That it is His joy that finally and fully gives us back to Himself, to ourselves, to each other. That it is His joy that upholds us.

And the only thing left is to serve His table, and be given to His joy. To go do this and share in Christ together.

And what else am I saying except that we are not ready for His joy? That we are not ready for what this is all about?

We are being prepared by Christ himself for His gladness. Prepared by His forgiveness and His company for His joy. Prepared by His dying and rising for His coming. Made ready by death and resurrection for His return. Prepared by His gospel and Spirit for His fellowship.

We are on a journey toward being given. A journey that begins as we sit at His table and ends as we learn to serve it.

To give regard and be given in His name and given to His joy. To see Him more clearly as we give a more Ordinary Hospitality. Learning His gentleness, entering His grief, sharing His gladness.

This regard. This sign of His cross, our share in His joy. This anguish and light. This place we meet.

3

A CRUCIFIED HEART

Another word for faith, hope, and love

I BELIEVE IN A CRUCIFIED HEART. Faith, hope, and love. The fear of the Lord. That undeserved stillness.

I BELIEVE WE CAN BE RESCUED, LED, AND GIVEN. But it's hard to believe in something after all we've lost, all the trouble we're in, all the lies we've been told. And when pride is often our only shepherd.

Somewhere between the ages of eighteen and thirty-four I had a bad boss in the evangelical world, a mentor who almost devoured me. He was a pastor and I wanted to be a pastor. I wanted to be a pastor because I loved people and I had been told I had a gift for preaching.

I have to be clear—it was spiritual and emotional abuse. The kind of thing that's hard to prove, and that lawyers don't care about.

I'm trying to not be exact about who he was or the time I spent with him. We only need his silhouette walking between the pages of this book, to protect him and to protect myself from him.

He was a mentor back when I didn't know what ministry was or what I was supposed to be doing.

When I left my bad mentor, I left the things I was made to feel were his to give: honor, security, purpose. Things I was told were being kept safe for me even as he kept them from me.

When I walked away from him, I walked away from who I was going to be and what life was going to be like. I had to leave the idea of myself as a successful person. All the honor, security, and purpose I was going to have. I had to crash and burn on an idea of myself and take on a life as a nobody who didn't know what was going to happen.

From a would-be pastor to a kinda sorta chaplain.

Leaving was horrible. My wife and I left friends and coworkers without any real explanation, mostly because it wasn't safe to explain. Leaving was horrible, and the only thing worse would have been not leaving. And the only thing that made it worth it was not having to be around him.

When I say "bad," I mean that word in all its fullness.

My first memory is of him at a bar. I visited his church and he took me and some other folks to a local brewery. And we laughed and I paid attention to him and this is what I thought of him:

Very intriguing, overly harsh, almost benevolent. My first memory is of him at that bar. He was sly, pugnacious, funny, combative. But also he appeared to actually care what you were saying, when he wasn't telling dirty jokes.

But when I picture him, I picture him in his windowed office. Him swiveling from the computer monitor toward me in glasses and a plaid shirt. A forest and lawn in the window and him swiveling toward me. When he swiveled he always looked like he had just read a funny joke on a website he couldn't tell you about.

I would always sit in that office, on a faux leather couch that squeaked and slumped too far down. It was usually a little too cold. The faux leather couch was next to a bookcase that just had binders on it. It all happened in his office.

His office was to the left of the front door, and directly past the copy machine. I remember.

He styled himself as "coach"—tough, chewy, resilient, brusque, cynical, knowledgeable. World-weary but not tired, battle-hardened but not broken down. The kind of man who could get things done and turn you into the kind of person who got things done.

He made you feel honored that he would spend time on someone like you. He made it clear you should feel honored. That it would be wrong to not feel honored.

He made it clear by his brusque manner and the roll of his eyes. He made it clear he didn't really have time for idiots like you.

But then with a great sigh and a hand over his heart, he made it clear that he also had God's own heart for idiots like you. With that great big sigh of mercy.

He made it clear that way. That was how he made it clear you were both in and out. A nobody and a somebody. Very special and complete trash.

That was his way of making you understand that everything that came after, no matter how dismissive, cruel, wrong, or bizarre, was to be understood as part of that gift, the gift of his time and attention. Even when it was weird and wrong, you were supposed to feel honored.

It all happened in his office. All those weird talks were in his office. He would blow you off when he saw you elsewhere. But the office is where he paid attention to you. The office was where you received the gift of his time and attention.

All the weird and wrong stuff was to be thought of as part of the gift of his time and attention. Part of his long-suffering love for losers like you. And if you didn't understand that, the reason you didn't understand it was because you were an idiot.

You realized, looking back, that *idiot* wasn't really a word describing you. It was a word for anyone he did not find looking back at him in a full-length mirror.

You were an idiot because that was what he said you were. He was a gift because that was what he said he was. And he got to decide what things were. It was a position he took. And he did it with the authority he had, the trust he built, and the words he used.

And you went with it because he was a pastor and you didn't know what a pastor was—only that you thought you wanted to be one. You went with it because he was respected and you wanted to be respected. Because you loved Jesus and loved people.

He was a pastor, but looking back it would be better to have not had one. It would have been better to have not pastored. He had a whole backlog of people he mentored. And I can only say I don't know anyone who is better off for having known him. If you were around him you got steamrolled by what he turned out to be like. After years with him you looked in your own mirror and saw the ghost of what you used to be like. You saw that you had been slowly destroyed by the gift of all that time and attention.

There was a pattern. You were in his office once a week, for hours at a time. He gave out that time and attention sacrificially. He worked hard, he plowed diligently. And his gift to the church was the young men he'd ruined. His gift to the church was the damage he'd done.

After you'd been chewed up by the gift of his time and attention, he declared you incompetent with a tragic, faraway look in his eye. And found someone else on which to bestow the gift of what it turned out he was like. He would find someone else to pastor.

THE THING THAT WAS HARD FOR ME, the thing that I still haven't got over, was just how clear it was from the very beginning that he just wasn't that great of a guy. He was a cartoon person, too loud, braggadocious. He was obviously ridiculous. And he made it clear by that shove and swagger, by the way he talked, that he just wasn't that great of a guy.

It wasn't that he was mean, or critical. It was that he consistently practiced disregard. A man who enjoyed dismissing others, discrediting, invalidating everyone. And he did it with the authority he had, the trust he'd built, the words he'd use.

Later I asked a friend, "Why did we stick around so long when it was pretty obvious from the beginning that he just wasn't that great of a guy?"

I stuck around because I thought I had a calling, because I wanted to be a pastor and I didn't know how to be a pastor. Because if I was going to be in ordained ministry I was going to need a mentor. Because he was the only one around. Because he was loud, well-known, and apparently effective.

And because he promised to teach me so much. And he did. He gave me the liturgy, rhythm, and song of this denomination. The ones I still use. The ways good news still comes to me. He gave me thorough, rigorous instruction in the liturgy, rhythm, and song of this denomination. The rich treasures of the Christian tradition. He taught me to love them. How to love liturgy, how to love Scripture. The good news coming to us in gentle, lapping waves. Good news coming to us through rhythm, liturgy, and song. The hymns he taught me to love I still love. The liturgy he taught me to love I still love. I learned so much. I really did.

He had so much to teach me. And he did. But most of what we did was talk in his office.

He was not someone you contradicted or made fun of or advised or pressed or told he was wrong. But it was his delight to contradict, pressure, criticize, and dig into you, to be almost openly horrible, and to get away with all of it because he was loud, well-known, and apparently effective. To get away with all of it with the authority he had, the trust he'd built, the words he'd use.

And so he was an obvious ass, but his office was also the place where he winked, nudged, and intimated that lurking just behind the obvious fact that he was an ass was a deeper secret—that lurking just behind all that bluster and swagger was the fact that he was a really great guy. In his office he told you he was a true shepherd and a tenderhearted man. With that really big sigh and a hand on his heart he made it clear that he simply would not be spending this kind of time on a loser like you unless he was a really great guy. He kept pointing to his heart when he sighed in his chair, pointing to the really great guy deep deep down, the tenderhearted shepherd that you just hadn't met. The really great guy he still had you thinking he really was, and that you kept waiting to meet. The one you kept waiting to meet in his office.

I KNOW THESE WORDS ARE STRONG. It takes me a long time to find the words for what people are to me. The words I have are the way I see things and how I live with things. I think we can only live as well and see as clearly as the words we have. And so we need to find the right words.

And I struggle to find the words to say what he is to me. I can feel my sentences getting mean. I can feel them wanting to get mean, waiting to get back at him. I flatten them out into beautiful little trails of thought, and they curl back into little jabs, little punches at his silhouette. My sentences are little monsters that want to take things back and make things right. It's like they want to change what happened and change how hard it was, and they just can't.

I have to withstand the edge I still have, to fight what comes natural, that impulse toward vengeance, retaliation, hostility, spite. Even if only in my choice of words. That impulse toward taking things back and making things right.

These are the words I have found for him: that my pastor was not just a bully and a liar, even with all the endless bullying and lying. That my pastor was not just a monster, even with all that ruining and devouring. That my pastor was not just not that great a guy. That my pastor was more mysterious than just not that great a guy.

That my pastor was a stranger to himself, and a god to others. He was a child who'd lost something, and a god who was going to get it back. Those are the words I have now: a ruined god, a frightened child, a tortured soul. A stranger to himself. A god to others.

And he was that way because of pride and lies and trouble and loss. All he'd lost, all the trouble he was in, all the lies he'd been told. And the pride that had been his only shepherd. All the pride and lies he couldn't withstand.

It's taken years to get there—to just get to that. All that time to just get those few words.

And with those words it is not that I've unlocked some kind of compassion for him so much as that there's only one kind of person to me now: a wounded, selfish, bullied, troubled person. Someone dealing with all they've lost, all the trouble they're in, all the lies they've been told. With pride their only shepherd.

Someone who must be cleansed and presented. Someone who needs a feast and a table.

That is the compassion I have on him: that he just wanted to be okay, that he was a wounded, selfish, bullied, troubled person who just wanted to be okay.

A ruined god, a frightened child, an utter stranger. A stranger to himself, a god to others.

That was what he was. The only horror was what he would do to be okay. And what he would do to be okay was destroy you. Destroy you if you left, destroy you if you stayed. Destroy you if you stood still.

Destroy you in that office. It all happened in his office. Destroy you with the words he had, and what he could do with the words he had.

I look back and say this to myself: The saddest thing wasn't that he was mean to people. The saddest thing was that he wasn't able to be good to them.

That's the saddest thing I have to say about him. That he didn't know how to be a gift to others. That he wasn't able to be given. That he only knew how to take from them. Only knew how to trap and devour them.

He was trapped. To be a gift to others was not something he could do.

That's the saddest thing I have to say about him. But the most important thing to say about him was that he was wrong. Wrong about what ministry was, wrong about what it's like. Wrong about what a pastor does and why.

Wrong about what this was all about. And that's what crushed him, and crushed me. The wrong idea of what this is all about.

I REMEMBER HIM, AND WRITE ABOUT HIM, because I have to.

If this is the story of the work I do now and the Person this is all about and the few things I still believe in, then we have to meet my pastor, however briefly. I think we have to take a look at him in that office.

I haven't seen him in many years, and haven't wanted to. But I remember his face. He wasn't ugly or handsome but it seemed like he had a face that you just weren't going to forget. A face cut out of granite. A big movie screen face. Not like an actor's face on the screen but like the movie screen itself. Big, looming.

His face seemed too big for that office. His life seemed too big for that office. There was a severity and grandeur and authority to a face like that. It was a face that seemed to push reality right toward you. A big granite face ready to impose its will on the world.

I remember he was strong and stocky but not in a way that would make you think he'd ever been athletic.

I remember how he laughed, that high cackle. His coarse jokes. His way of looking at things.

I remember he could be a lot of fun to be around. We had a lot of fun talking in that office.

The office was where we talked, and how I learned his way of seeing things.

I remember how he sat in that swivel chair and divided everyone in the world into two great big piles. He did it with his mouth. He did it with his words. Two piles: a pile for winners, a pile for losers.

He lived in a big, fake, made-up world full of only winners and losers, successes and failures, somebodies and nobodies. That was his world. You discovered that world just by hearing him talk. You were in that world just being in his office, just by having him as your pastor.

And if you were with him you were in his world of winners and losers. And in that world you were his to build up and shape and name, his to bless or curse, his to qualify or disqualify.

And the point, it seemed, of being mentored by him wasn't to grow in Christ but to make sure you got in the right pile. The winner pile—you wanted to be in the winner pile. You wanted to be declared a winner in that office.

He loved to talk trash in that office. His body would loosen up, and relax. You knew he was about to talk trash.

He would talk to you about people in the denomination who were supposed to be his friends and tell you everything about them. He would reveal to you that although he loved them a lot, they were all idiots who could not be trusted or fixed. And as he talked about them, it was like their name had been written on a chalkboard and was now being crossed out.

Canceled, disqualified. Right there in the office.

And you knew, with that story he was telling, that those friends of his must have done something wrong, must have gotten themselves into the wrong pile. You couldn't be a pastor if you got in the wrong pile.

When he told stories about his friends in the denomination he looked like a disappointed surgeon, looking down at the flat-lined corpse of a loser he'd tried to make a winner. Like he'd like to help but he just couldn't, because it was just too late. Just look at them. It was too late. They were already a loser.

A great big sigh. A hand over his heart. That swivel chair. And that verdict over them, that nothing could be done. Not even by someone with God's own heart for losers like them.

And you did not want to be like his friends in the stories he told you in his office. All those losers he tried to breathe life into with great, big gasps of abusive air. All those losers he couldn't turn into winners. You did not want to be like that. You wanted to make sure you were in the right pile. The winner pile.

But the problem was he made sure you never knew which pile you were in.

He tried to make sure you never knew how he really felt about you. And he tried to make sure you never really knew how you felt about yourself.

He kept you guessing in his office. He always had a way of making you feel like there was something else you really should have been doing that day, that week. Even if you did exactly what he'd told you to do. You were never just okay, there was always something wrong with you, or with what you were doing. You were always in trouble.

Your ministry was never bringing in enough people, he said. Your preaching was good but not great, he said. You had a few talents but you were a liability in a lot of other ways. You're not the worst, but you still might be a loser, he seemed to say.

And when you told him about someone you liked or appreciated he would tell you a story about that person, a story that revealed that they were actually a loser.

He would swivel in his chair and point that big movie screen face toward you, point it right at your trembling, eager credulity, making his pronouncements with that occasional high cackle. You would squeak and squirm around on the faux leather couch.

Sometimes the things you said made him laugh and nod, and you were glad that the stupid things you said weren't stupid. But often, when you were baring your heart after one of his probing questions, he would make one of those buzzing sounds with his great big lips, throw you a contemptuous glance, and with a flick of the wrist it was as if what you had just shared—what had just revealed about yourself, your ideas, secrets, passions, interests—had been swept into some imaginary trash bin on the floor.

All those passions, interests, ideas, secrets—right there in the loser pile. All those parts of you crossed out, right there in his office.

Oh no, you thought. If all my passions, interests, ideas, and secrets are in the loser pile, am I in the loser pile?

The wrong pile, you thought. The wrong pile. How did I do it? How did I get here? How did I end up in the wrong pile?

THE FACT THAT THE WORLD WAS BOGUS didn't seem to matter. The fact that his logic had been cast down by the cross of Christ didn't seem to matter in his office.

The fact that I knew better didn't seem to matter. It was as if even though it wasn't true, it was true anyway. It somehow got to be true anyway.

I once met a woman at our church. She was tired, pretty clearly just passing through. And she said, "I'm stuck in an abusive relationship. The thing is, I have a master's degree in psychology. I studied people like him. He tells me I'm a stupid piece of shit, and I know it's not true. I know what he's doing. But the thing is, it's like it doesn't matter. It's like it doesn't matter that it's not true. It's like it gets to be true anyway."

It was like that.

His was a fake, made-up world. It clearly and obviously went against all gospel logic. But it was real anyway. The stench and curse and undertow of it was still there. It was stupid and it was real. It was stupid and you were too smart for it, but he did it anyway. He did it with the authority he had, the trust he'd built, the words he used.

You thought you were tough, savvy, and ready. You thought you could handle this obvious ass, and maybe if he wasn't your boss and you weren't his student and you weren't completely new to ordained ministry and maybe if your career wasn't in his hands then maybe you could have withstood an obvious ass.

Maybe you could have. But it didn't matter. You were being slowly ruined in his office in ways you wouldn't have words for until later. Things were happening in this office you didn't have words for. Things were happening inside you you didn't have words for.

You thought you were tough, you thought you were savvy, and maybe you were but you just got ruined anyway.

The world created in his office stayed with you. That way of seeing things, that way of looking at things, was first an undertow, then a pull, until you were just some small thing in his hands.

He was discerning. He studied you in his office. And if you worked for him for any length of time, he saw what you were vulnerable to and what you were embarrassed by.

You went to his office when things were wrong. You told him what was wrong, and he would ask good questions and listen. And the pay-off was that he had all your secrets and you were some small thing in his hands.

The more he knew about you, the more you began to feel that way—that you were some small thing in the palm of his hands. And it felt both good and wrong. He would mention the tender secret things he knew about you in odd ways and at weird times. He would use those things to spin you around when he thought you were going the wrong way, or to pull the rug out from under you when you thought you were going the right way.

And all in that office.

You were a small thing in his hands and it felt both good and wrong at the same time until he made it clear he was willing to clench his hands and squeeze his hands until you were just a crunching sound and some juice running through his fingers.

He would swivel around and crush you in his office.

When you defied him, he would throw that contemptuous look at you and refer you to that pile of losers. He would do it with his words. He would tell you about the careers he'd ruined—that a word from him to his vast network of loyal friends in the denomination would end what you'd been working toward and the life you thought you'd have.

And you remember thinking, "Who brags about ruining careers?" But all I had to do was look at him there in this office.

This guy. This guy does.

THERE'S A LONG HALLWAY in my mind, and at the end of that hallway there's a room. That room in my mind opens to that office, and to a specific moment in that office. That room is the moment he turned on me and became what I'd never seen before. The room was my introduction to that place, that place where the worst happens, and nothing makes sense, and everything falls apart.

If he would've been even just a little less awful in that one moment, I would have never left. I could have even become a successful pastor. I would have stuck around, gutted it out, prided myself on my long-suffering love, and finally been driven insane.

But in that moment he was awful to me in a way that made it clear who he was.

Whenever I go into that room, I know that I will feel confused and bad. Not just a regular confused and bad but more like shattered, ruined, breached, compromised, fragmented. Tenuous, fading, incoherent. Crumbly, flickering, helpless.

I only go in that room to visit someone—the person it happened to. I go there to visit that prior version of myself. This is my sad Grandma.

It has taken a long time to talk about that room, and to have the words to say it casually. It's taken years to be able to sound casual about what he did.

When I go into that room, and step back into that office, and remember when I got crushed, what I remember is that big looming granite face.

I remember telling that big granite face that our last few conversations had been discouraging. That his latest criticism had been harsh, erratic, baffling.

That it seemed like everything I did was fine until suddenly everything I did was wrong.

My ministry was fine except it was tanking. My preaching was fine except it was horrible. My leadership was solid except it was completely incompetent.

I said it was confusing. My performance sucked except it was fine except that it sucked which didn't matter because it was fine.

The goalposts kept moving. I was always almost about to be in trouble for something.

He had a special way of making ominous clouds appear in a clear sky. He would put a dark undertow in clear waters.

I said I didn't like this dynamic. I asked for a different way forward.

I said that and then his face changed. I'd never seen someone turn on me before. Eyes bulging, hysterical. He became a new creature. Something that had to eat to live.

What was the look on that big granite movie screen face? It was the look of a ruined god, a frightened child, a complete stranger.

It was like a ruined god and a frightened child and a complete stranger were all fighting for control of his face. Like a laser beam had been pointed at his face and he was becoming a new organism through the agony of science.

His face suddenly seized by despair and anguish. His big looming face contorted with wounded honor, sudden terror, unconquerable loathing.

While the ruined god, the frightened child, and the complete stranger fought for control of his face, he was saying things, his face hysterical, bulging, like he was being crushed, like an undertow was yanking him down to depths.

He said he didn't feel safe with me. That I was attacking him.

He said I made him dislike himself. He said I wasn't stable. He said I would flounder in ministry. That my ministry would crumble. He said that it hurt him that I didn't want to be his friend. He said if I got a job at another church he would put a stop to it. He said he was the only person who believed in me and everyone else thought I was crazy.

There it was. The trash pile. That trash pile feeling.

There in his office.

I didn't understand: I was in the trash pile but I couldn't leave. I was a piece of trash but I had to stay. And a dark, creepy, ruined, gross, violated feeling took over.

I'd been crossed out, discredited, nullified. I was that trash pile, there in that office. He'd done it with his words. I was in that office and I was looking at all the distress and satisfaction and repulsion on his face, and hearing all his words. He was cruel and terrified and disgusted and taking pleasure.

I see it now. I see it now with these few words I have.

He was desperate and repulsed and scared and pleased. All those things in that one big face. I'd set something off. I had activated some tremendous overwhelming force inside him. He was at the mercy of this tremendous thing inside himself, and this sudden violent cruelty was the attempt at holding onto himself.

I see now that big waves were crashing inside him, some undertow was pulling him down, and he was flailing. Everything was falling apart and he was flailing. He was dissolving and drowning and falling apart and this cruelty was the only way to hold onto himself. Drowning me so that he would not drown.

I don't know why, but I know that. I remember that.

I see it now—cruelty, vengeance, retaliation, spite, manipulation, defiance—as part of a painful longing, the attempt to hold onto himself in the midst of all the things coming toward him, all the things going on inside him. Just to be okay. To be cruel so he would have rest.

We are no match for the things going on inside us, and so we start the flailing. When we're busy defending ourselves, taking things back, and making things right, what I see is that we're flailing. Drowning and flailing. Just trying to be okay. Being cruel so we can have rest.

He was drowning me so he could live. Holding onto me like a life raft so he wouldn't have to feel what it didn't seem like he could live through feeling. At the mercy of all the things coming toward him, all the things going on inside him.

Flailing because of all he'd lost, all the trouble he was in, all the lies he'd been told. And pride, his only shepherd. Wounded, selfish, bullied, troubled. But the only horror was what he was doing now. The only horror was what he would do to be okay.

I can see him now in that office. All the roar and bluster. And I see the saddest thing wasn't that he was mean, or braggadocious, or rude to people. It's that he wasn't able to be good to them. He was trapped. I'm in that office, looking at the face of someone who was drowning, and I can see clearly what life is like, and what it's not about.

IT IS WEIRD TO REALIZE you've been abused like that. It all feels hazy and gross and confusing and wrong. You don't want to overreact. You think that maybe it's okay, except you know it's not and that you've been violated. Something sacred has been violated.

I guess I thought abuse was about people being mean, but it's about power and safety and fulfillment, it's about hunger and feeding and feasting. It's about what people will do to be okay.

And to be feasted on like that, fed on like that, to be used like that by someone with that kind of pleased and distressed look on his face felt creepy and gross and wrong. And it made me feel cursed and ruined and stuck.

When he said that, and when his face did that, I felt something break in me. A thread in me snapped. It was, I realized later, the thread that held me to the world and the world to me. Some fundamental trust I had with people, places, and things snapped. It was my introduction to that place where the worst happens and nothing makes sense and everything falls apart. And I was in that ocean now, in this wild country.

And when that thread snapped, chaos came into my life. All of sudden there was no such thing as seen or safe or fed. And I didn't even know what I was supposed to want. Life became a place without words. I only wanted rest.

When that thread snapped, I felt two things that were born at the same: the serpent called chaos and disaster, and the feeling that I was now a crumbly, flickering, and helpless thing.

The serpent called disaster was the expectation of catastrophe, the anticipation of calamity, the premonition of collapse. The fact that life was not essentially stable and that anything could happen now. The serpent was disintegration, confusion, incoherence.

The serpent was close at hand, and has never really left, coiling in and out of all the moments I was in.

Soon after, everything I did felt like stepping out on a branch that was going to break from underneath me. Everything I did felt like walking on a tightrope that would be snipped off at one end.

In a moment I got crushed, and the thread snapped, and I was in that ocean, and there was no longer a sequence of moments. That moment got to be every moment after. That moment got to swallow every moment after. That moment was the trapdoor waiting underneath every other moment, the gap every other moment fell into.

Something about it was the end of me ever expecting things to work out. I only expected the serpent now. And why?

I've had to think about how he held my life in his hand. He taught me how to love Scripture and liturgy. How to preach this good news. My spiritual life was in his hands.

He knew my wounds and vulnerabilities. My mental illness, my emotional hang-ups. I had told him more than I should have about how I was doing. My emotional and psychological life was in his hands.

He was well-known and respected in a denomination with a limited number of jobs and opportunities. His opinion mattered. He had connections. My career and my financial life were in his hands.

IT WAS A RELATIONSHIP THAT HELD together every aspect of my life. He had created a world where only he could be trusted.

When the thread was cut, everything was suddenly gone.

I began to feel tenuous all the time—distant, fragmented, shattered, fragile, barely there. Distant, dissolving, fading. Crumbly, helpless.

It is hard for me to know what to make of that sensation, that flickering, fading, exposed, crumbling, dissolving, tenuous, fragile feeling. In one sense I don't want to feel that way, and yet the key to getting better was the willingness to feel that way. The only thing that felt like me was my willingness to feel that way. A willingness to feel that crumbly, flickering, helpless feeling.

I would walk around and live my life as that crumbly, tenuous, helpless thing, as that vulnerability, as that flickering, catching sight of the shadow of the great serpent of chaos and disaster in the fault lines of everyday life.

I loved him, I trusted him. He taught me that good news. He taught me that Simple Rhythm.

I just never thought he'd do that to me. And I didn't think it would change everything so much. I was a grown man. It shouldn't have changed so much.

And so he cajoled and cursed and blackmailed and berated in that office.

And that was it. Except that a stillness joined me as he spoke. A stillness joined me and stood against him. A stillness joined me as he cajoled and cursed and blackmailed and berated. All I had was that stillness. An undeserved stillness that said there was no way to make things right and that I didn't have to. That stillness put an impression on my heart. And a verse: "Because I live, you also will live."

I don't know if there's anything more unpleasant, more distressing, than that feeling of confusion, disaster, falling apart. A combination of twilight zone and free fall.

When I go into that room in my mind, and step into the office, that big looming face is all I see, and confusion and disaster is all I feel.

And the only thing I can take into that room is an undeserved stillness. An undeserved stillness that says I can't make it right and that I don't have to. An undeserved stillness that says, "Because I live, you also will live."

HE CURSED, CAJOLED, BERATED, BLACKMAILED. He did it with his words. And when he was done, he asked how I felt. I said I felt crushed and betrayed.

He said I shouldn't feel that way, that he didn't want me to leave here feeling crushed and betrayed. With that sigh, that hand on his heart, that condescending tone for idiots and losers he'd just devoured.

Later, in his office again, when his granite face had returned to its normal look, to that almost benevolent look of contempt and calm and mild dismay, he told me that all he'd done was what a spiritual father would do. That he sensed a stubbornness in me that had to be broken.

I told him what he did was wrong, that I wanted mediation with the authorities in the denomination. I wanted some denominational authority to step in and negotiate this because this just wasn't right.

I told him that in his office. He turned his face to me.

He said no one had ever, ever tried to take him out like this, tried to get him in trouble like this. He told me I was putting him in the woodchipper, taking him out to the woodshed. He made it sound like I was abusing him.

He told me that if I reached out for help, for mediation, it would be taken as a red flag on my mental decline. If I told people what he'd done, I would be the one in trouble. He reinforced what he had already said: that everyone knew I was crazy. He was the only one who still supported me.

He told me to understand it this way: that he did this because he loved me, that what I had received was mercy. Law and gospel. Tear you down to build you up, tear you down to build you up. I should feel the sweet burn of it and be grateful.

I was made to feel that, through the means of grace of his abusive leadership, it was Christ Himself who had done this to me. That it was Christ Himself who had crushed me in His hands.

Jesus made you feel like that.

The gospel makes you feel like that.

He told me that what he had done was grace. That he had done what a spiritual father would do.

I thought of my real father. A man so tenderhearted that he soared over his broken hips to run to me after a disagreement. How he nurtured, guided, shepherded, cared. How I was never made to feel that I was some small thing that would be crushed in his hands. I was never made to feel I was to be feasted on, destroyed, devoured. Not once. Not ever.

I remembered my father. All his gentle, costly care. All the regard and gentleness. His fiercest song to me.

Not long after that meeting with my pastor-spiritual father, I remembered my real father.

And I left any kind of ordained ministry and took on a life as a nobody. A life as a caregiver. A part-time evangelist and a kinda sorta chaplain.

It was painful because I had to leave everything—almost every relationship. People I loved, things that were flourishing. I had to leave, and I left.

When I left, and wasn't his to boss around, he made sure I was his to discredit. He did it with his words. I couldn't stop that mouth, and man—did that mouth love words. Words, words, words to pull a fake made-up world back together. Lies, lies, lies to pull a bogus world back together.

Talking, talking, talking. In people's ears, calling up local pastors, local ministries, telling them what he thought they needed to know about who I was. He spun a relentless, tireless web of words make it right.

Forgetting what words are for. That words are for what's true. That words are for those few good things that life is still about. And the Person this is all about.

He told people either things he made up or things he only knew because I had told him in confidence. I stopped trying to keep track of what he told people.

His words changed the way people looked at me. They changed what was possible for me in ministry. He did exactly what he had said he would. And he did a good job of making sure I was a nobody.

I had to remember my father a lot around then. I had to go home a lot.

When I got confused about leaving, or saw how hard it was, I remembered my father's gentleness, his regard, his song. The man who soared over his broken hips to reconcile with me. Sometimes all I needed was to hear his voice on the phone. And I kept going.

What is the payoff of long-suffering love? Of gentleness? We give people a song. My father gave me a song by which to leave somebody. That was his gift to me.

Sometimes I wonder if I'll see my old mentor at the grocery store. Squinting, pushing that big granite face toward some kind of cereal. I will look at that big granite face, and nod and say hello. And get back to what I was doing.

I have to remember that lies work until Judgment Day. Then the Lord comes back, and we all sit down at a table, and the truth is told, and it all gets sorted out.

I TRY TO NOT GO INTO THAT ROOM. I don't want to stay in that office.

But I'm there all the time anyway. A lot of things feel like being in his office.

Hard conversations feel like being in his office. Difficult relationships feel like being in his office. Change, transition, and uncertainty feel like being in his office. Conflict and tension feel like being in his office. Ordinary life feels like being in his office. What is trauma to me? Trauma is a rupture, the gap everything else falls into.

The whole world feels like being in his office. Because his office was the introduction to that place, that place where the worst happens and nothing makes sense and everything falls apart. And I was in that ocean now, in this wild country. A place of pride and lies, trouble and loss, chaos and disaster. Where there are no words. And I don't even know what I'm supposed to want.

It's a room down the long hallway of my mind. The room opens into his office. I only go in there to feel confused and bad. To feel like it's over. It's an office that feels like the end. It's the office where I get crushed.

I only go to visit someone: the person who was crushed.

It's not a room I want to go into, but I can. The best way for me to go into that room is by writing. When I write about it, I have words.

Words to hold up to the things that happened. The words by which I see things clearly.

Words that are a kind of hospitality to myself, and a fierce light in that room. I feel like the Lord gives me these words. Words I found about the table in this place. This place where the worst can happen and nothing makes sense and everything falls apart.

Those words I found are the words I bring into this room.

Words for who my pastor was, who I am, and who God is. I come into the room with the promise of who He is. With these words I feel like Christ is a fierce light I carry into the room. A light held out to myself. Christ with me by the promise of good news. Christ there by announcement. A fierce light, a tender, stubborn regard. This strange sign of Christ. To go see that prior version of myself. To go do this and share in Christ together.

I go into the room with a small candle, a small light. An odder, kinder, gentler light. This light; this tender, stubborn regard.

The light in that room is the Lord Jesus Christ. I hold out this most basic, tender sign of the reality of Christ, the forgiveness of sins, the homecoming offered only in Him. I hold it out to this prior version of myself. I hold it out to him by writing these words.

The light of regard held out to him. This way to be with him, this gentler way for us to be together. To share in something and see each other clearly. The One we share when we share in something. The joy we offer, the joy in offering. The Person this is all about. A life in Christ that includes me seeing him, him seeing me.

This regard. This fierce song, this strange sign of Him. A fierce song, a gentle light that says nothing that happens can change what life's about.

Even in this room, even in this office. This brighter light, this darker shade of blue, this deeper note of rest. Even in this office. All my longing, sorrow, and patience in this one place. This place we meet.

This light makes it feel like I can be in this room. And I know if the candle is there, remembering won't crush me.

Remembering what happened. The bitter feast of others. The bitter feast of exactly what happened.

We are strangers to ourselves. We don't visit ourselves often. Perhaps we don't think we'll come back from the visit in one piece.

I go into the room with that light that won't go out. I see my boss, his big granite face, gearing up to yell at the prior version of myself. Getting that pleased, terrified, disgusted, enraged, sated look on his face. I see my younger self sitting there, telling his boss that the way he does things is discouraging. Trying to be nice about it, trying to be aww shucks about it. I see my boss rear up, swivel his big movie screen face toward that John. And I somehow pause it all. I pause it all and I hold the light out to my younger self. And I talk to my younger self.

"Hey, buddy."

"Who are you?"

"I'm you from later on."

"Why are you here?"

"I'm here to see you. I'm here to visit you."

"What's that in your hand?"

"It's a light that won't go out."

He nods. "What's happening to me?"

"You're about to lose, John. You're about to lose real bad. And you're in a lot of trouble. And you've been told a lot of lies. And there are no words for all you've lost, and all the trouble you're in, and all the lies you've been told. There are no words right now."

"Can I fix it? Can I stop it?"

"No, buddy. You're gonna learn what it's like to lose."

"What's he doing?"

"The things you don't really have words for now. Some classic emotional blackmail, spiritual abuse, gaslighting."

"Why?"

I hold out the light of regard to my paused boss, too, so that we both see him—the ruined god, the frightened child, the complete stranger. That disgusted, desperate, pleased, terrified look. The wounded honor, the sudden terror, the unconquerable loathing turned to me.

"It's the only way he knows to be okay."

"But my life is in his hands. I've been working for years to be a pastor. I've gone to school for it. He took me under his wing, he said he'd turn me into a pastor. He said he'd look out for me."

"I know."

"What's he going to do?"

"He's about to put his thumb on your face and grind you into the dust."

"Why?"

"So he'll be okay."

"Will he get away with it?"

"He'll definitely get away with it."

"Is anyone coming for me? Will anyone help me?"

"No buddy, I'm sorry. No one's coming."

"No one's coming?"

"In a little while, in the middle of what he's doing to you, you'll feel a stillness. You'll know is God with you. It's a stillness that says you can't make it right and you don't have to. You'll hear a verse in your heart: 'Because I live, you also will live.' "

"And that's going to be it?"

"That's going to be it."

"Will it make it better?"

"Only in ways you won't have words for till later."

"So you can't make it better?"

"No. I can just be here with you. I can just visit. I can just come to see you."

"And will that make it better?"

"I don't know."

"This conversation isn't really happening is it?"

"No, buddy, not really."

"It's an imaginative construct, isn't it?"

"Yeah, something like that."

"But you'll come to see me?"

"Yeah, I'll come to see you."

"Can I come with you?"

"No, I'm sorry. This is your life. This moment is yours."

"Will you come back to see me?"

"Yeah, buddy, I'll come back to see you. That's what I do now."

"What's that? You're not a pastor?"

"Not really."

"But you seem nice, you seem better. What are you?"

"I'm a sorta kinda chaplain. A part-time evangelist. I visit the crushed."

"And I'm one of the crushed?"

"Yes, buddy. You're one of the crushed right now. You're the first one I have to see. You'll get crushed here, and then you'll get crushed there, and then you'll feel crushed everywhere."

"What's it going to be like? What will I lose?"

"The floor drops out. An ocean comes in. An abyss opens up. Honor, security, purpose, all suddenly gone. Confusion and disaster. The twilight zone."

"And I lose?"

"Ground into dust, baby. Ground into dust."

"How will I handle it?"

"Oh, not well. You're gonna be hurt, scared, and upset for a very long time."

"And so the world just ends?"

"Kind of. But the world ends all the time."

"What will I do then?"

"You'll be in this ocean, out there with all you've lost, all the trouble you're in, all the lies you've been told, and pride as your only shepherd. Or at least a pride that seems like your only shepherd. You'll be in a wild country. You'll be in an ocean. You'll spend your time looking for solid ground, for a table in this place. A table that makes it right."

"But it's all right because I end up getting to be you?"

"Maybe. It's all right, and it's not all right. Sometimes it's both."

"But you'll come back?"

"Yeah."

"And you'll bring that light with you? The one that won't go out, so it's not so dark in here? You'll bring that brighter light?"

"I'll bring that light with me."

"And you'll hold it out so you can see me?"

"I'll hold it out so I can see you."

This prior version of myself turns to the big, paused granite face. Then he looks at me.

"What would you tell him now? If you could do it all over again?"

"I'd turn and look at the face of a ruined god, a frightened child, a complete stranger. With the fear of the Lord and means of grace I would turn my face to the ruined god, the frightened child, the complete stranger. I would turn my face toward all his flailing. And I would say, 'Sounds like you got a lot going on.' And then I'd leave."

"Maybe next time, right?" He smiles.

"Maybe next time."

THE LORD HAS PUT A CALLING ON MY LIFE: to go and visit the crushed. To go to my sad Grandma's house.

To go and see the ones who lost. To visit the people the worst has happened to. To take a light that won't go out. The tender, stubborn light of regard. To go do this and share in Christ together.

To go out and take this quiet sign of Him. This most basic, tender, and visible sign of the reality of Christ, the forgiveness of sins, and the homecoming offered only in Him.

This regard. This sign of His cross. This share in His joy. This anguish and light. This place we meet.

The light is when He gave Himself, and the light is when we go and see each other.

This gentler way to be together. To share in something, and see each other clearly. The joy we offer, the joy in offering. The Person this is all about. The One we share in when we share something.

To go out there with these few strange signs. With all my longing, patience, and sorrow. This tender, stubborn regard.

Our regard is the anguish and light. Our regard is the place we meet. To honor, uphold, and just be there.

To give regard, and be given in His name. And given to His joy. To see Him more clearly. As we offer a more Ordinary Hospitality. This word about the Word. This radiance of His feast. This invitation to His table.

How far do you take a light that won't go out? The further out, the fiercer the song, the more tender and stubborn the light.

I come out of that room, out of his office, with a vocation, a calling.

I am a part-time evangelist, a kinda sorta chaplain. A chaplain and evangelist who offers the ministry of presence to the crushed. To honor and uphold by just being there. For the goodness of the thing itself. For the deep gladness of just being here.

I go into his office and come out remembering that the Lord asked me to sing to the crushed, to sing a song about His table, the song by which He gathers the crushed to Himself. To people who've lost more than they can bear without any sign of Him.

Even if it's just a sign of a sign of a sign.

It's a sign of a Christ who is gentle with the crushed, who grieves with the crushed, and who gives them back their gladness. Who has news for them, a feast for them, a table for them.

Where does that mistreatment go? Where do all the losses go, unless they are all taken into His own body? The Son of God crushed with us, taking all we've lost, all the trouble we're in, all the lies we've been told. Taking the pride that's been our only shepherd. Taking all those things into His body. And dying and rising on the third day with the scars of all those things in his hands. Dying and rising with all of it. His song to us.

This brighter light. This cleansing, provision, and rest. That is the news, too.

What else can our losses hope to become? What else can Christ turn them into, if not longing? If not anguish and light? If not joy? If not gentleness, grief, and gladness?

Out here where we've lost. Out here where there's nothing we can do. Where there's nothing left but to share in who He is and what He's done. Where there's nothing but who we are at this table.

O Lord, teach me how to sing.

Your fiercest song. A more Ordinary Hospitality.

A more Ordinary Hospitality is the hardest work I've done. To be a friend to the crushed, when often you don't feel like you're doing well enough to be a friend.

To see how far you can carry a light that won't go out. To see if there is a song good enough to summon the ruined and the dead. To see Him more clearly. To offer only those things that cast His light. To learn His gentleness, enter His grief, and share His gladness.

The further we go, the fiercer the song, the stranger the sign. The more tender and stubborn the light.

We give regard, we come alongside, and we make places of rest. We work with His joy, and we are given to His joy.

We learn His gentleness, enter His grief, and share His gladness.

THIS IS OUR INHERITANCE. This is our song. Regard, company, places of rest.

These quiet signs of Him, quiet signs that this news is true. A hospitality we take out into the world. What we can give the crushed. These costly graces. Offering those things by which Christ gathers His people to Himself.

To tell them we are helpless sinners, honored guests, and humble servants of the Sabbath rest offered only in Christ. For ruined gods, frightened children, and utter strangers to be cleansed and mended and presented and become themselves again. I believe that. It happened to me.

I TRIED TO GO TO MY DENOMINATION, to the people who take care of these things when these things happen.

It turns out denominations don't like the word *abuse*. It's a word that makes them feel like they're in trouble. So they start looking around for other words, words that don't make them feel like that, words that make them feel like they're not in trouble.

I kept trying to tell the denomination about my pastor. For a long time they said it sounded like a generational gap, different leadership styles. That he was just old school.

And I thought, "What kind of school did people go to back then?"

When things got worse, and I told them how much worse they were getting, they said the things you say, like, "He must be under a lot of pressure," and, "He must be going through a lot."

Yes, I thought, spiritual abusers must have it rough these days. Got a lot going on. Groceries, kids, doctor's appointments. It's rough out there for spiritual abusers. Not like the old days.

I went to my denomination, sat in their offices, and was made to understand the boundless compassion and concern denominations have for powerful men who do horrible things because they're under a lot of pressure.

As I sat in their offices and smiled and thanked them for taking the time, what I kept hearing was that stability and success are more important than how we treat people.

When the abuse became overt, unquestionable, unambiguous, I sat in their offices while the denomination shrugged, admitted that, indeed, blackmail and spiritual abuse did not sound good at all, and with the utmost moral seriousness told me I was free to leave.

I couldn't believe it. I get abused, and I have to go? I get abused in his office and I have to find a new home?

I couldn't understand it. We were all grown men, looking at hard facts. I wasn't a nobody. I'd been in this denomination for a while, in charge of a substantial portion of the church's ministry while training to be a pastor.

Clear blackmail, threats, intimidation, spiritual abuse. Multiple complaints made by me and others over years and years.

But they couldn't see it that way. It wasn't possible for it to be understood that way.

Abuse was a nightmare. Abuse was very inconvenient. Abuse meant trouble, and trouble meant they weren't going to be okay. And so abuse couldn't be abuse. It couldn't be abuse because abuse would mean they were in trouble.

I could see their faces, these men I talked with. Their faces said, "It can't be abuse. Because abuse means we're not going to be okay."

This denomination had been my spiritual home.

I had always been a loner and had only had a few things to belong to: a college group I went to, a special needs camp I worked at. I was by disposition an outsider. I knew, by then, that life had more meaning in groups. Life had more meaning if there was a way to be together. If you were in a group, then meaning, purpose, and fulfillment were closer at hand. Meaning, purpose, fulfillment were in the things you were doing with other people. Meaning wasn't an abstraction or even a longing; it was the very things you were doing together. The One you share when you share in something like that.

There are few things like becoming a part of something. Like having a village that helps the world and takes care of itself. And I thought this was my home.

The place where I'd hear this good news. Where I'd learned this Simple Rhythm. Where I'd learned a simple life with this good news.

I was telling the denomination that our home was under attack. I was telling them bad news. And I was so gullible. I couldn't see it clearly: I was the threat. My testimony was the threat. Getting abused by an effective leader and trying to get help makes *you* the threat. You don't have bad news, you *are* the bad news. You are the thing that must go away.

Because if they are loud, well-known, and apparently effective, then they represent the denomination. And if they're in trouble, then the denomination is in trouble. And the denomination doesn't want to be in trouble. The denomination can't be in trouble.

Because, it seemed then, denominations don't exist to love and serve the world. Denominations exist to love and serve denominations.

I left their offices and realized that there's something worse than all you've lost and all the trouble you're in and all the lies you've been told. What's worse is when it doesn't matter.

And I just couldn't understand. If abuse was what it was, if abuse is what it is, then why call it something else? How can the truth be an enemy? If the truth is the truth, doesn't it have to be a friend? Isn't the truth the ally of the Truth?

I think I had it better than most, though. I was not silenced by my denomination. I was just ignored. I was told I could leave.

What was so hard was that this was a denomination that prided itself on taking a bold stand for Christian orthodoxy. It had an evangelical swagger. The swagger that prides itself on holding the line against the titanic forces of such and such.

And maybe they did take that big, bold stand. But it was as if they took that bold stand and became a bunch of people who didn't want to lose. Took a bold stand for God and then became a bunch of ruined gods and frightened children.

I didn't understand what I understand now—that a denomination is a bunch of wounded, selfish, bullied, troubled people who are just trying to be okay. A denomination is a ruined god, a frightened child, a complete stranger. It has its own honor, its own terror, its own unconquerable loathing toward correction and change and instability.

My denomination was like a person—the only horror was what it would do to be okay. And what would it do? It would look the other way. It would find something else to look at.

If your story is a threat to its honor, security, and purpose, then your story can't be understood as true. There is just not a way for it to be understood as true. There is too much for it to lose if what you said is true.

Or, perhaps more painfully, the people we bring charges against are people we love, people we care about. People we've laughed and cried with. People who've been there in hard times and been there in good times. And we don't want it to be true that they've done these things. No one wants it to be true.

My denomination didn't crush me. It did nothing to me. I guess that was it. It was just simple neglect. It just withheld presence. It just left me and moved on. My denomination didn't crush me; it just wouldn't look at me. It just never gave regard, company, or a place of rest. It just never gave me a sign this news was true.

I want to tell my old denomination: if you could just see the Look of Those Transfigured by those costly graces of regard, company, and places of rest. The Look of Those Transfigured is more important than whether we win or lose.

How could I tell them now? That we don't control outcomes. That our concern is what we offer. That a more Ordinary Hospitality is more solid and real than any premonition of doom, more solid and real than the worst that could possibly happen.

That these offerings cast their own light and strike their own deep note of rest. They are their own announcement.

I have friends still in this denomination. It was not that people in the denomination didn't care. A lot of people did.

And so I don't have any clear targets. Just a denomination. It was the denomination itself that didn't know how to care.

A denomination with its own way of doing things. A denomination: what happens when we get ourselves together and call ourselves something.

What happens when we get together, it seems like the world confirms again and again, is that we begin to make moral concessions for the good of the group's survival.

I'd like to think my denomination was a special kind of awful, but I don't think it was. I think this is what happens when people get together and decide to call themselves something.

It always seems to me like we get together and call ourselves something and become something worse. I don't think that's true, but that's what it seems like.

Individuals who can be forgiven become an entity that cannot. We become what we can't stand, the intolerable, the unacceptable. And I keep looking around, wanting to be mad at this thing called a denomination and realizing there's only other people, only what other people do when they get together and call themselves something.

I have a hard time trusting people and an even harder time trusting what happens when people get together. It doesn't matter how much you love those people; when they get together they become something horrible. You just can't trust any group of people to not be horrible.

Or maybe it is all more mysterious than that. Maybe a denomination, or any group at all, is a paradox.

Denominations are home to the sacred and the unacceptable, the beautiful and the inexcusable. A place to belong to, a horror to run from.

The denomination said that what he did was wrong, and not right, and not good. They believed me, and it still didn't matter. They believed me, and I was still a threat.

They believed me. They believed he had said that and had done that. It was just that he was under a lot of pressure. It was just that he needed a break. It was just that it was a tough season.

He's only overtly abusive when he's under a lot of stress. He only blackmails people when he's feeling down.

But they didn't say what it was. They didn't tell the truth: that it was heresy, that it was false worship and treason, to crush in your hands the people made in His image.

This denomination that had given me the good news, and this Simple Rhythm, didn't say that. A denomination that gave me this Simple Rhythm wouldn't say that it mattered what happened to me.

So I'll have to say it:

It is heresy and blasphemy and treason to devour the vulnerable. To crush in your hands the ones made in His image. It is heresy to not honor and uphold and welcome. To practice disregard.

A denomination that knew what was going on. A denomination that kind of just stood there and let it all happen. A denomination that both knew and didn't know, that both understood and couldn't understand. That believed it happened, but just didn't think it mattered all that much.

I WALKED AWAY FROM THE PASTOR and the denomination and took a job with an ecumenical outreach organization.

I took a job as a kinda sorta chaplain. I didn't really know what the job was. I didn't know if it was a job that would last. It was low key; it was just something people thought I'd be good at.

But I didn't know if I wanted to be an evangelical at all. And if a pastor crushed me, and a denomination turned its face away, the last thing I wanted was to be a part of an evangelical movement.

And the last place I wanted to be, right as I was starting, was at an evangelical missions conference.

This was the missions conference I would have a vision at—not that I knew that as I got into my dad's old truck and headed to the conference center in jeans and a baseball cap and a big floppy flannel.

What I call my big, relaxed clothes. The clothes I could wear because I wasn't a pastor now: that cap, those jeans, and the big floppy flannels—my consolation in the land of sin, death, and the devil.

Their sweeping abundance, their disheveled grandeur, the way they hung down my big lumbering body: a consolation, a hospitality toward myself. A tender stubborn regard toward myself.

Because it didn't matter anymore. There was no one to impress now.

Jeans, baseballs caps, and big floppy flannels were a goodness I'd found. Big, relaxed clothes my only consolation. They made me feel like I was going to be who I was. That I got to be who I was wherever I was. That nothing that happened got to turn me into something else.

People wear their big, relaxed clothes when everything's been settled. When the day's over and there's no one to impress. Big, relaxed clothes are what you wear when you are at home. What you wear when there's nothing left but who we are at the table.

I wanted to look like someone who was at home wherever he was, at home with himself and the world wherever he was, wandering around Walmart or standing in line at McDonald's. Someone whose life was what's in front of him. Someone who has a few things to do and no one to impress. Someone who's taking it easy, wearing those flannels, getting that sausage biscuit.

I'd just been abused and abandoned, and I was at a conference at a big convention center and I didn't really know anybody. And I liked that. I like to go in places and just walk around, a little bored, a little sad. In my big, relaxed clothes. Just looking around.

I got to the convention center and the missions conference was having a worship hour in a big auditorium, and there were lots of lovely people there. You could tell they loved Jesus and that Jesus loved them. It seemed like a real thing. And you could tell they loved Jesus because they had that big gaping wondrous look on their face that you get when you love Jesus. A look on your face that says that the look on your face is just not enough to express how much you love Jesus. The look on your face that says you don't need anything but you love everyone and you're fine with whatever's happening.

I'm not making fun of that look. It's the look I get on my face sometimes. Sometimes, if the sun is shining and I'm not careful, I'll get that look on my face.

They were lovely people. At another time, I might have even wanted to talk to one of the people who had that look on their face.

But I had been abused and abandoned, and had just started a job I had no idea how to do. And so I went and laid down where no one was.

I was on the highest row, at the very back, where no one was, where I knew I wouldn't have to say even a single word to someone with that look on their face.

I thought I would be bored and sad at the missions conference, but what I *was* was overwhelmed.

The things I heard and saw arrived in my head like explosions. Guitar riffs, big crying voices. And all the things people said—interruptions, advice, ideas, requests, encouragement—I felt them all as disruptive and violent.

I felt like I was being yanked around left and right.

I was tired of being friendly and social. I was tired of being an evangelical Christian.

I was at an evangelical missions conference and I just felt ruined. Confused, bad. Fading. Incoherent.

And felt that all this was the worst kind of nonsense.

I was at a missions conference, and so far it was full of lovely people who were very loud and very persuasive. Who gave compelling testimonies. Who loved Jesus and wanted to make sure you loved Jesus.

Did you love Jesus? Did you? Did you love him like this? Don't you know you should love Jesus? Why don't you love Jesus? You should love Jesus, and if you should love Jesus why don't you love Jesus?

The people there were a coiled spring, ready to enforce Christianity: encouragement, exhortation, enthusiasm, advice.

All I could hear was the clear note of force, coercion, manipulation, domination, pressure. That clear note behind it all, of being made to feel like you can't say no. The clear violation of Ordinary Hospitality.

I called it blowtorch evangelism. Evangelism as trap and ambush. A hard shove through an open door. Evangelism without gentleness or respect.

All that energy for the kingdom felt like being bullied. It stymies me still.

It wasn't enough to announce what is true. It had to be enforced. It wasn't enough to offer good news. We have to attack them with it. All those lovely talks from lovely people felt like that hard shove and an ambush. Pushing, pushing, coercion, pressure, strong arming.

Trying to make something happen.

Why don't you love Jesus this much? Or like this? Why don't you love him enough to do this? Or this? Or this?

All this bullying. An optimism I've always felt as cruelty. People's faces stuck in a spooky grin. An optimism that said, "We can get rid of hard feelings when we know Jesus loves us. We don't have to be hurt, scared, or upset if Jesus loves us. Did you know that? Did you? Did you? Did you?"

Something I've always had a hard time with: people who've never met themselves, who've never faced their loss. Who don't know that they're hurt, scared, and upset.

And yet who still believe God has put a special call on their life to tell people what to do. Strangers to themselves, gods to others.

A bunch of ruined gods and frightened children who said they loved Jesus. Who said I should love Jesus.

And optimism: always always always all that optimism. When all I wanted to do was cry and scream and tell them that—to the bullied and the crushed—it all felt like violence.

That if you've been crushed, all that optimism felt like cruelty. All that encouragement and advice felt like condemnation. All that charisma and persuasion felt like manipulation and betrayal. All that exhortation and enthusiasm felt like bullying and coercion.

I need to be clear this was what I *felt* it as. I'm not sure if that's what it was. I was too sensitive then. I am too sensitive now. But I'm sure I felt it as that.

You want to scream and say, "Everything you say helps just makes it hurt more." And tell them they have made you feel the worst feeling in the world, being pushed, pinned, controlled, devoured, made to feel like you can't say no. Not abuse—no, not abuse. But familiar, too familiar. Things that still felt like being in that room with that big looming face.

Was the missions conference as bad as I make it? As I remember? Memory is tricky, and I only have the silhouette. Even now the memory fades, and I can only speak of what I felt it as.

It may be that I was too hard on the missions conference. They were lovely people and meant no harm. I was sensitive and buried under everything that happened. But I still felt it as violence, even if I only felt that way because of what I'd already been made to feel.

Crushed by a pastor, left by a denomination, alienated from a movement.

Crushed by a pastor, left by a denomination, and a part of a movement I found incoherent, indecipherable. A complete stranger to what was happening. Confused, ruined, incoherent, fading.

I sat in the very back, not so much in rebellion as feeling ruined, alien, no longer part of this at all, exiled from all of it by everything that happened, so deeply cast out by this mentor, this denomination, this movement.

Feeling only the things I didn't have words for. Feeling only tenuous. Feeling only chaos. Feeling I was barely there, not even knowing if I was still there under everything that had happened to me. Feeling only that I was in that ocean, that place of pride and lies, trouble and loss, chaos and disaster. All I'd lost, all the trouble I was in, all the lies I'd been told. And a flailing pride my only shepherd.

A place without words, where there were no such things as seen, safe, and fed. Where I didn't even know what I was supposed to want, and where I only knew I wanted rest.

IT FELT LIKE CREEDS AND CONFESSIONS were the only things I had in common with the people who were at this conference and were going to be like this.

When people ask me what I believe, I tell them I believe all the dumb stuff.

"All the dumb stuff. Death. Resurrection. The forgiveness of sins."

It's the dumb stuff that is still beautiful to me. The dumb stuff is still what matters to me. It is the dumb stuff that has made the difference. The folly of the cross. The only thing I've been changed by.

I hold on to this good news: that Jesus Christ is Lord and Savior. That Christ has died, Christ is risen, Christ will come again. That the forgiveness of sins and the gift of the Holy Spirit has been offered in His name.

I just keep holding on to the dumb stuff. This feast right now.

I keep holding on, but holding on has never translated into energy, into a frenzy. It doesn't seem like it ever turned into what I saw other people doing.

It never turned into a successful career. It never turned into impressing a bad pastor.

I hold onto the dumb stuff, but holding onto the dumb stuff still just looks like me sitting in places in my big, relaxed clothes, walking around in my big, relaxed clothes, taking it easy in my big, relaxed clothes.

I believe in all the dumb stuff, but it still just looks like sitting here. The incarnate funk of just being here.

I believed in all the dumb stuff, but I couldn't handle coercion, pressure, force. I believed in all the dumb stuff, but I couldn't handle the hard shove and the ambush. The blowtorch. The swift dismissal, the disregard of that kind of optimism.

What must it be like to believe in things, to believe in people, in groups, in a movement? When I only believe He died and rose again. When it seemed to me there were only a few good things that were not lies. Only a few words about what this is all about. The table in this place. The Person this is all about.

I believe in this Person, these events. These few good things that were not lies.

I believe that Christians confess a Person and events. And I believe that when we hold fast to those confessions, we take hold of Him and He takes hold of us.

I believe that we are cleansed and presented by Christ Himself. All at once by His dying and rising, and day by day as we hear this news and offer a more Ordinary Hospitality. This good news comes to us in gentle, lapping waves—this repetition, this confession. Given back by this good news. News that cannot change but that continues to change us.

That's all I had. Those confessions, those creeds. That repetition. The confession of who He is, the announcement of what He's done. It felt like the only thing I had in common with the people who were going to be this way. I loved these words. I loved the goodness of these words—these few good words about this one Person. The Person this was still all about.

And I didn't understand. I knew they loved these words too. How can people who love these words do these things?

I SAT AT THE TOP OF THE AUDITORIUM, in the very back, not so much in rebellion as feeling ruined and scattered and fading and wanting to be alone forever.

I didn't know what I was going through. I didn't have words for all I'd lost, all the trouble I was in, all the lies I'd been told, all the things coming toward me, all the things going on inside me.

I was hurt, scared, and upset, and I just didn't know it yet. That is the only thing you can be when you've been crushed, abandoned, alienated. You can be hurt, scared, and upset. The important things are gone and all you have instead is loss. All you have are hard feelings.

All you have is chaos and hard feelings. Big waves called trouble and loss. A big serpent called chaos and disaster.

There are losses we don't even have words for yet. I'd crashed and burned on an idea of myself and I didn't even have words yet. The loss of who I thought I was, the loss of what life was going to be like.

I was in that ocean. I was beginning to feel more than I thought I could. Not just crumbly, flickering, helpless. Not just the serpent, the fault lines under everything. But now these great crashing waves, these great big things called hurt, scared, upset.

I was at the mercy of this tremendous thing inside myself. With a serpent that close, waves this big, how could I be OK?

We are tossed around by the hard feelings, and it's hard because there's no getting rid of them. There's no getting rid of them because in some sense they are you. They are your own soul groaning and crying for what's lost.

There's nowhere for those feelings to go because those big hard feelings are an important part of you. They're what you've lost.

Those big open wounds are yours. They feel like they might swallow you whole or drag you down and never let you back out. They feel much too big. And yet they are your hard feelings. They belong to you.

You're hurt, you're scared, you're upset. You've lost something. A loss of honor and regard, felt as shame. A loss of security and assurance, felt as fear. A loss of meaning and purpose, felt as despair.

I see myself at that missions conference. That prior version of myself, at the back of that auditorium after being in so many offices. I see him lying down in the very back. Hurt, scared, and upset, in his big, relaxed clothes.

By these words I see him clearly. As I write I hold the tender, stubborn light of regard out to a prior version of myself. A hospitality toward my younger self.

I know what he is. Hurt, scared, upset. Wounded, selfish, bullied, troubled. Ruined god, frightened child, utter stranger.

The trust he had with the world is gone, and the violation of that trust has made these deep, strange waters, these crashing waves, so that he doesn't even know what he's supposed to want. He only knows he wants a place of rest.

A place of rest there in the back of the auditorium. High up on the second level, at the very back.

The trust he'll need to become a part of things again has been broken, and that kind of thing doesn't just get put back together. It's gone in a way that doesn't get to just come back again.

And now with the serpent this close, and the waves this big, feeling this crumbly, flickering, and helpless, all he knows is this flailing pride. Trying to make things right.

I see him, and he is like his pastor. He is like his denomination. A ruined god, a frightened child, a complete stranger. And the question is, What is he going to do to be okay?

The question is, Is there a table in this place? Is there any kind of song? Or is it just this flailing?

I SEE THE PRIOR VERSION of myself and I want to tell him everything. I want to give him these words. To tell him the words I've found, tell him about the table in this place, the joy I found, the Person this still about.

I don't know that I can. But I know I can remember. I can remember being at the very back of that auditorium. There in my big, relaxed clothes. And I remember hearing this song, this song shaking the rafters of the missions conference.

I remember hearing that song. I remember how stupid and loud it was and I remember how beautiful it was anyway.

In the crushing, in the pressing, You are making new wine

There are those of us who believe all the dumb stuff—death, resurrection, the forgiveness of sins—and still cringe at the stuff we hear on the radio. At the pretty stuff like this.

And there I was, in the very back, crying. Crying without really knowing why. Crying because I still believed all the dumb stuff. This good news.

Crying because it's still the dumb stuff that was still beautiful to me, crying because it's still only the dumb stuff that has made the difference. Crying because I still believed all of it and only wished the people who believed it had treated me better.

I had the words to that song, the words shaking the rafters. And then, with it, suddenly, this vision.

A friend of mine at a table. That handsome, long-haired Mister Rogers. A man with acute schizophrenia.

A picture of him there, dark and blurry at the edges, with an odder, kinder, gentler light at the center so I could see him. So I could see him as he was: an honored guest at the very heart of things.

And with that vision, sudden, solid ground. A parting of the waters. A table in this place. Rest from pride and lies, trouble and loss. I was in my big, relaxed clothes and I was on firm ground and there was a table in this place.

A table with a friend of mine. An odder, kinder, gentler light.

A tender, stubborn light making it clear who he was and who I was. That's what I saw.

What I knew when I saw my friend at that table was that I really, really loved Jesus. I loved Him more than anything in my life. I loved Him more than pleasure and pain. I loved Him with all my anguished longing, with a sad, beautiful kind of pain.

And it was a love I didn't know what to do with. I loved Him because He was beauty and truth and goodness and I didn't want to miss out on anything that is beautiful, good, and true. I loved Him for who He was and what He has done.

He was that brighter light, that deeper note of rest. And there are things we only do because we love Jesus and for no other reason. Things we only do because of who He is and what He's done. Things we only do because we're honored guests and humble servants of His mercy. Things we only do because of who we are at that table.

And I knew what I wanted most was to be where He was. There was nothing left but to be here, to share in who He is and what He's done. Nothing left but who we are at this table. Nothing left but the offer of bread and the shining of light. This cleansing, provision, and rest. This place we meet.

I knew then that there was a feast to change what I want. A feast to change what I trust, and what I pay attention to. And that we are only as safe as what we want most. I knew that, at the back of the auditorium, and knowing that, I began to cry.

A wounded soul, with his thinning hair and his big, relaxed clothes. A wounded soul in the back of an auditorium. There to get away from other Christians, crying because he'd forgotten how much he loves Jesus. Crying because he heard a song, crying because he had a vision. A man who'd forgotten that Jesus is what was beautiful, good, and true. Crying because He'd heard good news again.

Given back by this good news. Good news that crucifies the heart.

There I was, in the auditorium, at the table. There I was, crying at the Table Called Mercy. This big, dumb, simple, beautiful table. And my friend. My crushed friend. His smile and his sad eyes. My beautiful, sad, crushed friend with acute schizophrenia. Handsome, long-haired Mister Rogers. There he was: cleansed and presented, and all of it a mending and finally himself again forever.

And I heard the words in my heart: "Will you serve my table?"

And with those words I'm crying, crying because there was something this was all about. Crying because I think I just needed to know I loved Jesus and that there was a Person this was all about. A place we're all supposed to be.

Crying at a table whose gift to us is faith. Whose gift to us is a Crucified Heart. Faith enough to cry.

Crying at a table that gives a Crucified Heart. That pastor, that denomination, this movement, made me feel far from that table, this Person, that word of mercy, so that I thought I was in an ocean. But here I was, at that table anyway.

And there He was, changing what I trust, pay attention to, and even want. Giving me back a Crucified Heart. Giving me a more Crucified Heart.

Maybe that was what I needed to know: no mentor, no denomination, no movement could change what this was all about.

THE NEXT MORNING I WAS IN THE DRIVEWAY of an Airbnb and I was going home and I felt terrible.

That solid ground, that table with my friend, that single word—it was all true. I knew it was all true.

But now it felt like it was gone. I was in the driveway of an Airbnb, pacing back and forth. A wounded soul, my thinning hair, my big, relaxed clothes, and the waves crashed right back. The serpent moved in close. An undertow pulled down hard. I was made to feel tenuous and flickering and incoherent again, and it didn't seem like there was a table in this place.

Not with all I've lost, all the trouble I was in, all the lies I'd been told, with this flailing pride my only shepherd.

It didn't seem like there was a way for me to get over myself unless I was at a table that makes things right.

And I was walking up and down the driveway of an Airbnb, and it didn't seem like there was a table in this place. It didn't seem like there was this brighter light, this darker shade of blue. This cleansing, provision, and rest.

That table was the word, but it was also the fulfillment of the word. Its own amen. It was the word but it was also its deepest note. It was a death that was also resurrection and return, a forgiveness that was also company and joy, a gentleness that was also grief and gladness, a truth that was also goodness and beauty, a cleansing that was also provision and rest. The table was the word, but it was also our return. There was nothing left but rest. All things had been overcome by that deeper word of rest.

I had been there. I'd felt it, and known that word was true. And now I was pacing up and down a driveway, restless, desperate, trying to make things right. I was flailing in a driveway, pacing back and forth like my friend with acute schizophrenia. There I was, the ruined god, the frightened child, the utter stranger.

How do I get back to that clearing? To the place where I felt solid and good for a little while? To the table that makes things right? To the place where I am upheld? To that deeper word of rest, to the fullest sound of it, to the deeper note saying that it had all been dealt with? How do I get back to the place where I knew I loved Jesus because He was beautiful and good and true?

I see my former self in the driveway of an Airbnb and I wish I could tell him. I wish I had these words for him. A few good words about the table in this place.

How's he somehow at the table even when it's like he's a million miles away. How he's at the table, but only by this good news. That He has to make a feast of this good news. The light that reveals Him, the bread by which He gives Himself to us.

Christ as near as the confession of who He is and the announcement of what He's done. As near as this good news and a more Ordinary Hospitality. As near as this good news and the few small signs this news is true.

I see the prior version of myself pacing in the driveway of the Airbnb. I see he has no words. I look down the long road he'll have to take, the long road he's taking, and I know it is my job to grieve those years for him.

To grieve those years as I write this book. To hold out the tender, stubborn light of regard to him as I write this book. My gentleness, grief, and gladness over this prior version of myself. All the sorrow I have for him, all the longing, sorrow, and patience I have for him.

Holding out the tender, stubborn light of regard. The regard I have for him.

This gentler way to be together.

This regard. This sign of His cross. This share in His joy. This anguish and light. This place we meet.

The light of my regard follows him as he paces, follows him on his long, slow walk out of pride and lies, through trouble and loss, toward meaning and rest. Follows him on his long, slow walk toward just sitting on the stoop.

I HOLD THE TENDER, STUBBORN LIGHT of regard toward his next five years, toward his long, slow walk through that wild country. His long, slow journey through that ocean. His long, slow journey toward that stoop. His long, slow journey from pastor to chaplain.

His long, slow journey toward wasted time. Toward a brighter light, a deeper note of rest. Taking hold of a Simple Rhythm, getting a more Crucified Heart, giving a more Ordinary Hospitality. His long, slow journey toward what it means to serve. His long, slow journey toward being given.

He doesn't see the five bitter years he'll have in this wild country. The years I'll have to grieve for him. This wounded soul, with his thinning hair and his big, relaxed clothes. The years I grieve for him as I write, with the tender, stubborn light of regard. The journey he's on and the words he'll find for why he'll stay.

WITH A SERPENT THAT CLOSE, waves that big, an undertow that strong, and a feeling that crumbly and helpless, he's going to start flailing.

It's a flailing called taking things back, making things right. A flailing called defending ourselves, proving ourselves. A flailing called just trying to be okay.

That is my compassion on him now: He just wants to be okay.

I can see him pacing up and down that driveway, and I know what he's saying. He's saying, "It's not right, it's not right, it's not right." What the pastor did, what the denomination did, what this movement's doing. "It's not right, it's just not right." And it's not.

And I want to scream at him through the waves and tell him what I know: that taking things back and making things right just isn't gonna happen. He won't find justice with his pastor, or get accountability with his denomination, or fix anything or make anything right. At least this time, there's no such thing as taking things back or making things right.

All too often there's no such thing as defending ourselves, taking things back, or making things right.

I want to yell through the waves and tell him in the driveway that there's no such thing as taking things back and making things right. There's only this flailing. I want to tell him what I know now—that there's only stillness or flailing.

I want to tell him that I wish I knew why it had to be this way. I want to tell him there's no such thing as taking things back and making things right. That the flailing pride only makes us drown more. That the flailing pride only gets us more ruined.

It's not right, and there's no way to make it right. At least not right now.

I want to tell him to find the table in this place. To take hold of a Simple Rhythm, get a more Crucified Heart, give a more Ordinary Hospitality. To stop flailing, and to be rescued, led, given.

To be rescued by His gospel and die with Him. To be led by His Spirit and rise with Him. To be given to His fellowship and share in the joy of return.

Because for him, for this prior version of myself, there's no such thing as taking things back, and making things right. There's nothing left but to share in who He is and what He's done. Nothing but who we are at this table.

To be rescued, led, and given. All at once by His dying and rising, and day by day as we hear this news and offer a more Ordinary Hospitality. I want to tell him, there in that driveway, that that's all there is. I want to tell him that that's all that's left.

I want to say, "John, find the table in this place. A table as near as this good news."

I want to say, "John, you're at this table, but only by this good news."

I want to say Jesus is as near as this good news. This light that reveals Him, this bread by which He gives Himself to us.

"John, you wounded soul. Pacing the driveway with your thinning hair, your big, relaxed clothes. John, cling to the dumb stuff. Take hold of a Simple Rhythm, get a more Crucified Heart, learn a more Ordinary Hospitality. Let it be enough."

I swim out to him as I write, the wounded soul pacing the driveway of an Airbnb. I don't know if I can get to him. I swim out to him and hold out the tender, stubborn light of this regard.

I swim out to him and feel the things he feels because they're what I've already felt. A serpent that close, undertow that strong, waves that big. Feeling that crumbly, flickering, and helpless. I swim out to him, holding that light in my hand.

"What is this?" he says.

"It's my light," I say.

"No, this." He points to the ocean.

"The bitter years," I say. "The wild country."

"For how long?" he says.

"More than a couple. Close to five."

"Will there be anything good?"

"A few good things. A few really good things. A wife who sticks with you, a few friends who stick with you, work you actually like. But mostly these are bitter years."

"What am I going to do?"

"You're going to have to find a table. You're going to have to learn how to sit at a table and keep a feast."

"What does that mean?"

"You're going to have to find a way to be with Jesus."

"What do I learn here?"

"The difference between flailing and stillness."

"When will I feel like myself again?"

"When you can be given."

"How long will it take?"

I don't have the heart to tell him, because the years are bitter years.

I don't have the heart to tell him about his long, slow journey toward being given, his long, slow walk toward what it means to serve. How long it takes to get to a stoop. I don't have the heart to tell him: "As long as it takes to sit on a stoop."

I don't have the heart to tell him that he's not ready to serve. That he cannot be given. He is not ready for joy. He is not ready to give regard, or to be given in Jesus's name, given to His joy. Not ready to see Him more clearly as he gives a more Ordinary Hospitality. Not ready to learn His gentleness, enter His grief, or share His gladness.

Not ready for what this is all about.

That's what I want to tell him. But I don't think he can hear it. He's too busy flailing. We're all too busy flailing. Too busy getting crushed by what life is like.

WHY IS HE NOT READY to be given? He has not really met himself. He has not faced his own loss. He is not ready to be gentle and grieve, to face the screaming loss of things without the benefit of pride and lies.

He is not ready to be cleansed by this news and presented as this offering. He is not ready to have pride and lies taken from him by this good news. To lose the pride and lies that have made him feel solid and good. We are never ready.

It makes sense. If you're by nature a sensitive loner, if your evangelical pastor has crushed you, if your denomination has turned its face from you, then all you have is a serpent that close, waves that big, and a self that weak. All you have is chaos and hard feelings. That's all you're left with. And who is ready for that? Who can face the screaming loss of things without the benefit of pride or lies?

That is the hardest thing to do: to face the screaming loss of things without the benefit of pride or lies. Losses that feel like they just might swallow us whole.

That is the hardest thing to do: to hurt and lose and feel and still be gentle. To still be gentle with yourself and others.

He is not ready to be gentle.

They were wrong when they said hard feelings are over now that we've started loving Jesus. All my life I felt like I trusted Jesus and kept looking around for all those good feelings I was supposed to get.

They were wrong when they said we can get rid of hard feelings by loving Jesus. That it means we don't we don't have to be hurt, scared, and upset.

All we can learn to do is to trust Jesus with things that feel bigger than us. To trust Him with the screaming loss of things, the loss of honor, the loss of security, the loss of purpose.

The stillness of waiting. The stillness of being at this table. At this table but only by this good news.

The stillness of waiting for Christ to clothe our shame, to walk us through fear, to end our despair. The stillness of waiting to see if he is going to give us back what we have lost. Who is ready for stillness? The stillness of not taking things back and not making things right?

Who is ready for a Crucified Heart? The stillness of only hearing this good news? It is an excruciating stillness, a terrifying stillness, a burning stillness. It is the darkest shade of blue. The foulest stench. This stillness called rescued, led, given.

But we have to stand with the screaming loss of things if we are to be given. We have to trust Him with the screaming loss of things. By His gospel, through His Spirit, in His fellowship. We simply have to, or else we become a stranger to ourselves, a god to others.

This Crucified Heart: the gift by which we hear this good news and stand with the screaming loss of things. A Crucified Heart: the gift by which we begin to grieve.

What's worse: being hurt, scared, or upset? What's worse: shame, fear, or despair? What is the biggest wave, the hardest feeling? The hardest loss?

For me the worst thing is to be upset. The worst thing is despair. To trust Him with how upset I am. When I'm in despair, when things just aren't right.

For me, it is always despair. If there is something this book is about, it's about joy as the end of despair.

This joy. The end of despair and the beginning of sitting on stoops.

It is despair that has been my companion all my life, as close as a brother. There's an anguish and torment, a wretched sensitivity that seems native to my disposition. A sort of unconquerable loathing I've felt toward life in general.

The suspicion I have always had that there is nothing that life is actually about. The sense that the futility of things is always close at hand. The sense that nothing matters, that everything is wasted. That it is all just rotten and foul. The seeming pointlessness of most of what we do.

I have had to come to terms with the fact that I just get upset sometimes, overcome by that miserable futility and unconquerable loathing.

That feeling of being stuck, blocked, trapped. I get upset and suddenly meaning is gone and the world just seems bothersome and radioactive and a complete waste. I get upset in a way that briefly seems to leave no room left for me. A despair that crashes in so hard and heavy that I didn't seem to be left on board.

Suddenly seized with a despair. Not so much frightening as pitiful. Not so much lashing out as sitting down, pounding the grass, and crying.

A despair that briefly seemed to extinguish the possibility of myself. Not kind of upset. Just upset. Upset in such a way that all I got to be was upset. Sitting down, pounding the grass, crying.

Despair was the greatest wave, coming suddenly, leaving me sputtering somewhere. And upsetness felt bigger than me, more than me. It felt like it would swallow me whole.

As a child, I was told I was usually chill but out of nowhere I was suddenly dramatic, melting down, over it, hysterical. Sitting down, pounding the grass, crying.

It was a brief, sudden fit of hopelessness. A pitiful anguish. Never violent, not a danger, just upset and suddenly wanting to be alone forever. Just a brief fit of anguish. A complete alien to life itself.

I'd felt despair in great waves as a child. It was hard to understand how as a child and as an adult the sudden loss of comfort, consolation, or pleasure could leave me so immediately devastated. The sudden lack of pleasure, comfort, consolation was an inconsolable loss. In that sudden vanished goodness everything around me felt worthless, pointless, stupid, futile. Radioactive, tedious, bothersome.

Suddenly seized with that despair. Suddenly stuck, blocked, trapped.

There seemed to be no way to account for this sudden loss. That life couldn't possibly be like this and still have any meaning.

It was things like this:

Seeing *Father of the Bride* as a seven-year-old child and crying that night when my mom came in to say goodnight and telling her I was crying because one day I would raise a child who would just leave me. The futility of doing all that if that's what happens. I couldn't handle the thought of it, the sudden vanished goodness. And with the sudden vanished goodness a kind of refusal, a defiance. A withdrawal. A rebellion. Life couldn't possibly be like this and still have any meaning.

Not if it was as rotten and foul as this.

Things like this:

Going fishing with my father when I was twelve and sitting in the grass, hot and just not able to handle it, this horrible, horrible thing called a vacation, this horrible thing called a good time. Just feeling it was all worthless, stupid, rotten, and foul to be doing this. To have to be doing this. Watching even the beautiful things and everything around me just turn into filth and trash because I was so tired and hot and over it. The futility of doing all of this if this is all that happens. That life couldn't possibly be like this and still have any meaning.

Things like this:

Seeing a child cry at Walmart when he's already tired and his toy is taken and seeing that in that loss he's inconsolable and feeling that I understand completely.

And with all those things a horrible unwillingness, a withdrawal, a final withholding, a refusal to become a part of things. A refusal to be given.

And now all that unconquerable loathing and horrible unwillingness felt toward church, toward being with other people, toward being with people again, toward the bitter feast of others.

A great immovable stone set between me and being with a fellowship of believers. That great immovable stone being the fact that I just don't want to.

Not if it is like this. Not if it means we get crushed by a pastor, abandoned by a denomination. Not if it means staring in blank incoherence at a movement I just don't understand.

The long road I was on was to find out if Christ would be the end of my despair. If Jesus would come closer to me than that despair. To see if Jesus would be the way I got over things. To see if Jesus was more beautiful and good than how upset I was.

The long road I was on was to find out if I could be given back to His joy. If there was a feast to give us back to God, ourselves, each other. If he would end my despair by giving me back to other people.

Could I be given? Would I be given? Would I have to be given?

Given to His joy? Cleansed and mended as I am given by Christ to others?

Can He end my despair, and present me on this stoop?

Can I be rescued, led, given, when nothing's right? When it's not right and there's no way to make it right?

4

A SIMPLE RHYTHM

Another word for a devotional pattern of Scripture, prayer, and service

I believe in a Simple Rhythm. One of those few good things that are not lies.

With a serpent that close, waves that big, an undertow that strong, a feeling that crumbly and helpless, I was headed into bitter years.

And I only had a means of grace instead of pride and lies. I only had good news: announcements, confessions, and promises.

I was at this table, but only by this news. Jesus was around but only in a weird way. Not primarily in visions that made you cry at missions conferences, but as a simple life with this good news. This long, slow walk with His Spirit. The Spirit: the One who makes it possible to believe in the gospel and somehow live as if it were true. Jesus was around but only by His gospel, through His Spirit, and to His fellowship. A simple life with His good news, a long, slow walk with His Spirit. And it was often no beautiful, firm thing.

It was hard to sit at that table, keep that feast, and hear that news. It was impossible, except that it wasn't. Except that the Holy Spirit does it. The Spirit makes it possible to believe in the gospel and somehow live as if it were true. Cleansed by this news, presented as this offering. And all through His Spirit, and all of it a mending.

A long, slow walk with His Spirit, who leads us from hearing, through prayer, toward offering.

The only stillness I found was born of hearing. The stillness called hearing. The stillness of not taking things back or making things right. If I was hearing, then I wasn't taking things back and making things right.

It was Word and Spirit that gave me back, so I could be still, so I could be quiet, simple, and gentle even when I was hurt, scared, and upset.

How to make it clear? That I was abused in an office. Had a vision in an auditorium. That I paced up and down a driveway. And then I sat in coffee shops and a sad, green truck for five years, learning this Simple Rhythm. This long, slow walk? Until I was ready for this stoop.

A long, slow walk out of pride and lies, through trouble and loss, toward meaning and rest. A long, slow walk with the Christ who walks with us by Word and Spirit. This long, slow walk we take together.

Five years learning to sit at a table, keep a feast, hear this news, count on a means of grace. Learning a simple life with this good news, a long, slow walk with His Spirit.

Five years waiting for Word and Spirit to deepen my trust in Him, shepherd my attention toward Him, and give me to others in His name. Five years learning it's going to have be enough to be with Jesus.

And it was completely unacceptable, and it was more than enough. It was possible and impossible. It was possible and impossible because of His Holy Spirit. The One who makes it possible to believe in this news and somehow live as if it is true. Who cleanses us with this news and presents us as this offering.

There is nothing in my life that has been harder than to sit at this table and hear this good news. Everything in your life is organized against a life at this table. Nothing in your life wants you to be with Jesus and deepen your trust in Him.

When I think back on the bitter years, I think of coffee shops and sitting in my sad, green truck. A cute local coffee shop with a nice friendly porch. A 2005 Chevy Silverado with a sagging roof, ripped seats, and pieces of foam falling off the steering wheel. A coffee shop and a sad, green truck where I kept this feast, heard this news, and learned this Simple Rhythm.

I think of the painful gradualness of learning to hear good news. To count on His means of grace instead of pride and lies. The excruciating stillness of hearing this news instead of taking things back and making things right. The excruciating stillness of the feast right now. Something you learn in coffee shops and sad, green trucks. Something you learn while sitting there and crying. Letting good news cleanse the pride and lies over time.

Pride and lies that want me to defend myself, take things back, and make things right. Good news that wants to give me back to God, myself, and others.

It felt like the only difference between stillness and flailing was a Simple Rhythm of Scripture, prayer, and service, a simple life with this good news. Good news coming to me in gentle, lapping waves in local coffee shops and my sad, green truck. Good news coming to me in rhythm, liturgy, and song. The ones my denomination gave to me.

What have I felt over this half decade? That there is somehow a table in this place. That I am at that table by this good news, coming to me in gentle, lapping waves, at local coffee shops and in my sad, green truck. This wounded soul, with this thinning hair, these big, relaxed clothes. Cleansed and mended. Keeping this feast, sitting at this table.

A Simple Rhythm of Scripture, prayer, and service. The coffee shops and the sad, green truck I sat in before work, before caregiving or chaplaining.

A wounded soul with his thinning hair. Learning, learning, learning: to be rescued by His gospel and die with Him. To be led by His Spirit and rise with Him. To be given to His fellowship and share in the joy of His return.

It took me five years, but I learned that Simple Rhythm. Five years in coffee shops and a sad, green truck. A wounded soul with his thinning hair and his big, relaxed clothes. Five years in that bitter country with my Simple Rhythm.

And I called it the Emmaus walk—what I also call the same kind of day. This Emmaus walk, this same kind of day, was based on the Emmaus story, one of the most famous post-resurrection stories in the Gospel of Luke, where Christ comes alongside the disciples, revealing Himself to them through the Scripture (what

I'd call hearing), walking with them as they ask questions and beg Him to stay with them (what I'd call prayer), and being with them as they cook a meal for Him (what I'd call offering).

The disciples feel their hearts burn (a Crucified Heart). And soon they return to the other disciples in Jerusalem.

With this story, Christ shows us the walk we'll take with Him.

The Emmaus story was foundational to the years I spent in coffee shops and a sad, green truck.

A daily walk I take with Christ who walks with me, who moves us from hearing, through prayer, toward offering, who cleanses us with this news and presents us as this offering, and all through His Spirit and all of it a mending.

All at once by His dying and rising, and day by day as we hear this news and offer a more Ordinary Hospitality. So that every day is the same kind of day, and every day is about Him, receiving Him, staying with Him, working with Him. By hearing, through prayer, and as an offering.

The Emmaus story, the Emmaus walk was my life in this wild country. It was the table in this place, this place where the worst can happen and nothing makes sense and everything falls apart.

Receiving Him, staying with Him, working with Him. By hearing, through prayer, and as an offering. Cleansed by this news, presented as this offering, and all through His Spirit and all of it a mending.

Abused in an office. A vision in an auditorium. Mended in coffee shops and a sad, green truck. Until I was presented on a stoop. On this long journey toward being given. A long journey toward what it means to serve.

THE SAME KIND OF DAY felt like all I got to work on, all I got to get better at. Before I went caregiving, before I went chaplaining, the coffee shops and the sad, green truck were where I got to work it all out. I'm not even sure I know how to say what it felt like. Getting better at it felt like getting used to it. The Emmaus walk: my life in this wild country.

It was five years in the same town, and five years sitting in the same place. But it was the only way I got somewhere. My long walk out of pride and lies, through trouble and loss, toward meaning and rest. The only thing that ever took me out pride and lies, through trouble and loss, and toward their joyful end, toward this joyful return. The only way I got to claim safe passage. The only way to get to the feast right now. The only way I could find the table in this place, in coffee shops and a sad, green truck.

I can tell you what it started to feel like. It felt like His crucified hand in mine. It felt like being held onto and taken somewhere with my thinning hair and my big, relaxed clothes.

What I also called mercy's solemn procession: receiving Him, staying with Him, working with Him.

Heading toward a deeper love of Scripture, a better kind of grief, a more Crucified Heart, a more Ordinary Hospitality. Into the pierced hands.

I take the same kind of day wherever I go. I carry that Simple Rhythm in my head and my back pocket. I go to coffee shops with a Simple Rhythm, I go into hospitals and car accidents with this same kind of day. The Emmaus walk—receiving Him, staying with Him, working with Him by hearing, through prayer, and in offering—this is my life in this wild country, and everything else is just what's happening. I carry it in my head, in my heart, and in my pocket. I have it on the side of the road and while the dentist tears open my mouth and while people are screaming at me. It'll just be the same kind of day, whatever happens next.

Hearing, prayer, and offering were the little things I could stand to do. I did them in that order. From hearing, through prayer, toward offering. One note after the other to lead me to the song of what I offer. Mercy's solemn procession: receiving Him, staying with Him, working with Him by hearing through prayer and as an offering.

Too often I think we separate spiritual disciplines, when to me it seems like a single rhythm, one long, slow walk, one single procession: the promises of Scripture becoming the attempt at prayer and the sacrifice of service. A hearing that is led in prayer and becomes what we offer, so that it is all the fulfillment of Scripture.

This Simple Rhythm, this solemn procession, this long, slow work of His Spirit, was a set order of liturgies and songs. It was the rhythm, liturgy, and song my denomination gave me. I didn't have a pastor, a denomination, or a movement or cause. Just rhythms, liturgies, and songs they gave me, in coffee shops and a sad, green truck. They are how I made a simple life with this good news.

I come to a coffee shop with a Simple Rhythm. I bring the same kind of day to a little coffee shop. This Simple Rhythm is kept in these little books I've made myself, made out of rubber bands, computer paper, and duct tape. Rhythms, liturgies, and songs that I turn into little books. Good news coming to me through rhythm, liturgy, and song. Scripture organized for the scattered mind.

Ugly books I made myself, with all that longing, patience, and sorrow, with all my gentleness, grief, and gladness.

This Simple Rhythm involves these ugly little books, a handful of gel pens, and a dusty old harmonica, all kept in a fanny pack. And words already kept in my mind and heart.

Good news—all the good news I can get. The light that reveals Him, the bread by which He gives Himself to us. All the bread and light I can get.

It looks like I'm carrying around junk. And I am. I am carrying junk around in a fanny pack, but I'm also carrying Jesus around. In my mind, I'm carrying Jesus around. Ugly books, gel pens, a dusty harmonica. How I'm used to being with Jesus. Mercy's solemn procession. How I walk with the Christ who walks with me. A Christ unafraid of my ugly books, gel pens, and dusty harmonica.

A thirty-four-year-old man, sipping coffee, holding onto muffins and gel pens. Breathing in deep. Learning to withstand pride and lies, to stand with hard feelings. Rocking back and forth, listening to quiet music, closing his eyes. Trying to keep this feast. To count on the means of grace instead of pride and lies. Trying to find the table in this place, the place where the worst can happen and nothing makes sense and everything falls apart.

At the coffee shops and in my sad, green truck, feeling so crumbly and helpless, so scattered, unresolved, tangled. Tenuous. At the feast and feeling ruined even still. Wondering if I'll drown in this ocean. Wondering if I'm still there underneath everything that happened to me.

Abused in an office. A vision in an auditorium. Mended at coffee shops and sad, green trucks. Until I arrived at this stoop.

Cleansed and presented. All at once by His dying and rising, day by day as we hear this news and offer a more Ordinary Hospitality.

To be rescued by His Gospel and die with Him, to be led by His Spirit and rise with Him. To be given in His name and share in the joy of His return. All at once and day after day.

Wash, rinse, repeat. Wash, rinse, repeat. How do you put five years into a montage? A montage of coffee shops? Sad, green trucks?

How does one long, sad montage begin to look like movement?

An order, a procession, and a sense of movement. The good news coming to me in rhythms, liturgies, songs. The good news coming to me in gentle, lapping waves. Coming to this wounded soul in his thinning hair, his big, relaxed clothes, his fanny pack. This good undertow.

Cleansed and presented. Receiving Him, staying with Him, working with Him, by hearing through prayer and an as offering.

Trusting in Him. Trusting Him with things. Entrusting myself to others.

A good undertow. The only good Groundhog Day.

I wake up now knowing most of the day is already spoken for. No matter how close the serpent, how strong the undertow, how big the waves, how crumbly and helpless I feel, I will still have this day. I will still walk in this procession. Receiving Him, staying with Him, working with Him. The world could end and I would still have the same kind of day. The world could end and I would still have a table in this place. The world could end and I would still keep the feast. With my fanny pack, my thinning hair, my big, relaxed clothes. In my coffee shop and my sad, green truck.

Cleansed by this news, presented as this offering. And all through His Spirit, and all of it a mending.

Somehow learning this: "With your constant love you led the people you redeemed; you brought them in safety to your holy dwelling."

A DAY AT A COFFEE SHOP and in my sad, green truck is like this:

I sit at that coffee shop with my thinning hair, in my big, relaxed clothes. They make big oatmeal peanut butter cookies here. I usually eat one of those cookies.

I eat a cookie and then I try to hear good news. It starts with a liturgy. The preached Word, the Lord's Supper, the good news preached and shown—now simply recited.

I take out one of the ugly books I've made. The words "Liturgy of the Hours" are written badly on the cover in Sharpie. Simple liturgies made up of a short confession, a few set Scriptures, and a few set prayers.

Keeping the feast by simply reciting this good news. That Jesus is Lord and Savior. That Christ has died, Christ is risen, Christ will come again. That the forgiveness of sins and the gift of the Holy Spirit has been offered in His name.

This good news coming to me in gentle, lapping waves. Unchanging news that continues to change us. This light by which we see Him, this bread by which He gives Himself to us.

I sit at the coffee shop or out on its sunlit patio. It works best if my mouth is moving and I can hear myself say good news, even if it means people are looking at me. The continual washing of the means of grace. Eating bread, seeing light.

Cleansed and presented. All at once by His dying and rising, and day by day as we hear this news and offer a more Ordinary Hospitality. Good news preached, shown, now recited.

When I'm done I take out the gel pens and another ugly book I've made myself. This ugly book has the words "Gel Pen Lectio Divina" badly written on the cover with a Sharpie.

With the Gel Pen Lectio Divina I sit with a single small passage from Scripture—a gospel, psalm, or epistle—and mark, illustrate, and illuminate it with a gel pen. I take out the verse numbers and make each passage fit on a single page. Each psalm or passage has its own page, separate from the passages before or after, so that each one is its own framed moment, its own tile, and psalm or passage is framed by its own white space and looks like a portrait. With the Gel Pen Lectio Divina, I go through each individual passage three times.

The first time through I mark what stands out or what I want to pay attention to with red pen. The second time through I use a bright gold crayon to color over what I've marked with red, sealing it in that Crayola wax. The third time through I color over what I've sealed with a crayon with a blue, purple, or pink marker. What I marked with a red pen and sealed with a bright gold crayon remains even when you color over it with marker. I use other markers to illuminate the rest of the page. Blue for longing, purple for repentance, pink for joy. The whole thing ends up looking bad. And it is. But they're sacred to me—the scribbles of a part-time evangelist and a kinda sorta chaplain.

It's how I can sit with good news and gradually let it have my trust and attention. The slow rescue of trust, the slow shepherding of my attention.

A simple life with this good news. On this long, slow journey out of pride and lies, through trouble and loss, toward meaning and purpose. A simple life with this good news. A long, slow journey we make with Christ.

Keeping the feast. Good news preached and shown, now recited and reflected on.

I take out one last little ugly book I've made myself. The word "Evensong" is badly written on the cover with a Sharpie. I also take a dusty harmonica out of the front shirt pocket of my big, relaxed clothes. At this point I'm not in the coffee shop. I'm in my sad, green truck. The Evensong book is made up of simple little Gregorian chants, easy old hymns that are just quarter notes. Good news preached and shown, recited, ruminated on, and now sung and chanted.

An ugly little book, a dusty old harmonica, my thinning hair, and my big, relaxed clothes. Wailing something simple and sad. A harmonica that made the bitterness of the last few years of my life sound beautiful to me. That can turn pain into sorrow and longing. That can make what I'm going through a song to the Lord. I make it wail. It sounds like wailing. And it is. A holy mess of sound that only a part-time evangelist and kinda sorta chaplain can make.

The kinds of sounds you make when you're hurt, scared, and upset. On a long, slow journey out of pride and lies, through trouble and loss, toward meaning and rest.

At the table by this good news. Trying to get to the feast. Trying to find the table in this place. Trying to hear this word. With a serpent that close, waves that big, undertow that strong, a self so tenuous, crumbly, and helpless.

Abused in an office. A vision in an auditorium. Mended in coffee shops and a sad, green truck. Until I arrive at this stoop.

These little ugly books, a pack of markers and gel pens, a dusty old harmonica. A wounded soul with my thinning hair, my big, relaxed clothes, my fanny pack.

What am I doing? Mumbling, scribbling, wailing? I'm at this table, keeping this feast. Counting on something, claiming safe passage. I am in mercy's solemn procession. Cleansed and presented by this news. Presented as this offering. And all through His Spirit and all of it a mending.

I put the harmonica down, take out my phone, and hop on Zoom. My parents and I and another friend or two are there. We do the Daily Office on Zoom. Reciting news again.

On Zoom I see my father's face. I learn small talk. We've done this for the last five years. We yik yak, then we do the Daily Office. This man who taught me gentleness, who soared over broken hips to reconcile with me. We talk, we discuss Scripture, we pray for each other, and then we log off.

I can't tell you how miserable I've been and still logged on to see my father's face and hear this small talk. Day after day, year after year.

To see my father's face and to give regard. This sign of His cross, this share in His joy, this anguish and light. This place we meet.

WHEN WE'RE DONE I get out of the sad, green truck and I often start walking. My thinning hair, my big, relaxed clothes. I move to the attempt of prayer. Trusting in Him by hearing, I attempt to trust Him with things through prayer. I try to trust Him with how hurt, scared, and upset I am. To trust Him with trouble and loss. To trust Him with chaos and hard feelings. To trust Him with all the things coming toward me and all the things going on inside me.

I say the Jesus Prayer: "Lord Jesus Christ, Son of the living God, have mercy on me, a sinner." The prayer is itself a summation of Scripture, the summary of this good news. I say the Jesus Prayer again and again as thoughtfully as I can, and then I go inside myself and try to withstand pride, lies, and trouble and to stand with those losses I can't get rid of. I try to face myself with that undeserved stillness. I fight the rush and push of the things coming toward me and all the things going on inside me. I sit with all these things as long as I can. Trusting Christ with what it's possible to feel, with how messed up life is.

The devil's condemnation—any signs of verdict looming over me other than the gospel.

Death's provocation—any signs of suffering and death and decay.

Sin's domination—any signs in me of taking things back or making things right or trying to prove myself.

Mind's intimidation—any signs of OCD, trauma, or depression as I know them.

Body's anticipation—any signs of stress or threat held in my body.

Soul's deprivation—any signs of shame, fear, and despair, of being hurt, scared, and upset.

Day's protestation—any conflict, tension, or setbacks of the day so far.

Moment's invitation—the world outside my skin; what I hear, see, and feel in the moment I'm in.

I try to sit with those things, stand with those losses. Not fix them, just stand with them, withstand them. I take this inventory and lift everything to Christ by saying, "Lord Jesus Christ, Son of the living God, have mercy on me, a sinner." I try to trust Christ with whatever I find.

I get back from the coffee shop, back from the sad, green truck, back from the walk, and I start my work. I move from the promises of Scripture and the attempt of prayer to the mundane acts of service.

Perhaps this is the beautiful thing the same kind of day has given me, this understanding—that there are a million things to do but only a few things I'm ever doing. The day at hand starts to look like another of those Lectio Divina tiles: a few small things I can stand to do. A tighter and tighter frame around each moment, like a movie zooming in on something, closer and closer. Until this messed-up life has blurred and zoomed into the task at hand.

I hear and pray and then I offer. The solemn procession leads me to the consecrated task at hand. And when I offer, there's only a few things I'm ever doing:

Taking care: eating, chores, exercise.

Having fun: book, game, craft.

Working on stuff: caregiving, writing, chaplaining.

The Lord has given me these few things to get better at, these few ways to be given: taking care, having fun, working on stuff. And only these few things to work on: caregiving, writing, chaplaining.

I go from coffee shops and my sad truck to the work I do. Ordinary tasks set aside by His means of grace. This solemn procession putting a tighter and tighter frame around the day. The tighter the frame, the richer the feast. Until this messed-up life is the size of the task at hand and the moments I'm in. These few things I can stand to do.

Taking care, having fun, working on stuff.

These few things could make up the craft of living, and could hone the craft of living by the fear of the Lord and the means of grace.

We hone the craft of living with good news and a Crucified Heart. With a Simple Rhythm, a more Crucified Heart, a more Ordinary Hospitality. A solemn procession to take us to the task at hand.

Held together by the feast right now. The table in this place. Good news and these few small signs this news is true.

We have these things we can offer, these few ways we can be given, and it seems to me the only thing to do is to learn to offer them, to get better at being given. To hone these few crafts, to hone the craft of taking care, having fun, and working on stuff. Held together by the feast right now. Trying to find the table in this place.

The consecrated task at hand—one of the few good things that are not lies. Those few good things you offer yourself to. Cleansed and presented by this good news. Presented as this offering. And all through His Spirit and all of it a mending.

This solemn procession is the only thing that ever led me to beautiful things. The slow rescue of my trust, the slow shepherding of my attention, leading me here, to the consecrated task at hand.

A long, slow walk out of pride and lies, through trouble and loss, toward meaning and rest. A long, slow walk toward what I offer. The vindication of this news, a long, slow walk toward what I offer. Toward my sign that this news is true.

Caregiving, writing, chaplaining, caregiving, writing, chaplaining, caregiving, writing, chaplaining.

"With your constant love you led the people you redeemed; you brought them in safety to your holy dwelling."

In these last five years I've made a lot of stupid little ugly books. Hundreds. I never really understood why I made so many. I wasn't really that good at it. It just felt like what I should I be doing.

But those little ugly books are the only montage of the last five years.

The artifact of those bitter years, and the time spent in coffee shops and a sad, green truck. The only thing that shows I was heading somewhere. The only thing that shows me this mending. That I was heading toward deeper love of Scripture, a better kind of grief, a more Crucified Heart, a more Ordinary Hospitality.

I started off watching videos on how to make them and trying to do what the videos said, using staples and a lot of cheap glue, needle and thread, computer paper, a cutting board. I'd take the rhythms, liturgies, and songs I saw trapped in the big, beautiful books my denomination used and put them into a small little Word document. Then I'd print, fold, and staple them into small, ugly little books that fit in my back pocket. I put these rhythms, liturgies, and songs into my back pocket. The rhythms, liturgies, and songs that were the only thing I had left, the only thing that still felt like mine.

I started off watching videos, but I pretty soon I started going my own way, making my own books. I suppose if I'm honest I didn't really want them to look good. I wanted them to look repurposed, like junk being pooled back together.

I gave these books to all my friends and family—friends and family who did not want them. Friends and family who were too kind to tell me they did not want them.

I kept making these books in my sad, green truck, the materials in a cloth Vera Bradley bag my mom didn't want anymore. The materials kept spilling out in traffic.

I kept making them between work and home, not because it was a new career of mine and not because people wanted them but because it felt like what I should be doing. I didn't want to fall apart. And something about making stupid ugly little books felt like just about the exact opposite of falling apart.

I could focus on those little ugly books when the serpent was close and the waves crashed in. When I felt crumbly and helpless at a coffee shop or in my sad, green truck, I'd sit there and make books. It was like a movie zooming in on something. My messed-up life would blur and zoom in on the task at hand.

Threading pages together again and again. Threading the books together was like watching this ocean become a table. It was like watching this messed-up life blurring and zooming in on the consecrated task at hand. I could make these books and stand with the screaming loss of things. All I'd lost, all the trouble I was in, all the lies I'd been told.

The books getting smaller and smaller. Tighter, simpler. Streamlined. A Simple Rhythm and a Crucified Heart. Good news and this deeper trust. Bound tighter, bound closer. Even when I was hurt, scared, and upset.

These books. This way to stand with my wounded soul, my thinning hair, my big, relaxed clothes, my fanny pack. A way to stand with the screaming loss of things, with how hurt, scared, and upset I was, and to bear the waves coming in.

Making better books. Bound tighter, bound closer. Sewing paper together. Needle and paper. A Simple Rhythm and a Crucified Heart. Good news and this deeper trust in Christ.

This way to be upset. This way to trust Him with how upset I was. This hospitality towards myself. This regard toward my own wounded soul. My wounded soul and I. This anguish and light. This place we meet.

My wounds and I met here: at the consecrated task at hand. At the craft table my sad, green truck had become. My wounded soul and I. This place we're supposed to be. This way to be together. This regard. This anguish and light.

This place we meet.

HURT, SCARED, UPSET, AND MAKING books at coffee shops and in my sad, green truck. Letting my hands tell me I'm going to be okay. Letting my hands tell me I would be upheld. Letting my hands tell me this is where I'm supposed to be. Letting my hands say, "I shall not die, but I shall live, and recount the deeds of the LORD."

Held together by the feast right now. A Simple Rhythm and a Crucified Heart. Good news and a deeper trust. Bound closer, bound tighter. Being more still.

How many relentless attempts until I arrived at this Simple Rhythm, the same kind of day? How many relentless attempts till I arrived at the perfect stupid little ugly book? The perfect set of rhythms, liturgies, and songs for a wounded soul to take out of his fanny pack. With his thinning hair and his big, relaxed clothes.

Now I make the books with an ugly, effortless ease. I don't even need scissors and glue. Just duct tape, thread, a hole punch, and a little time between things. My own book, my own thing sewn together. My own little braid of those two things: thread and paper, a Simple Rhythm and a Crucified Heart, good news and this deeper trust in Christ.

The books are smaller, simpler, tighter. Bound closer with Him, bound tighter with Him. Focusing down, focusing down, focusing down. Braided tighter. Bound tighter. Good news and a deeper trust. A Simple Rhythm and a Crucified Heart. This messed-up life blurring to the task at hand.

These ugly books scattered across my room, a strange sign of the reality of Christ, the forgiveness of sins, the homecoming offered only in Him. Ugly things made by someone who's hearing good news. Someone who's hurt, scared, upset, and at this table. Someone who's held together by the feast right now. A Simple Rhythm, a Crucified Heart. Good news and a deeper trust in Christ.

Making books because there's nothing left to do, nothing left but to share in who He is and what He's done. When there's nothing but who we are at this table.

I could feel even then that I was becoming weirder. You've got be careful when you make books in your sad, green truck. You don't want to look like one of those people who makes books in their sad, green truck. But there I was.

A mystery to myself. Abused in an office. A vision in an auditorium. Mended in coffee shops and my sad, green truck. Until I arrived on this stoop.

My office is full, too, not just of the stupid little ugly books but of the illuminated tiles of the Gel Pen Lectio Divina. I tear them out of the ugly little books I've made. The pictures are wild: that mess of gel pens, crayons, markers. I keep them—scores of them. Little illuminated tiles of this good news. Some beautiful, some ugly, some wild. Signs, signs, signs of this good news, of the reality of Christ, the forgiveness of sins, the homecoming offered only in Him.

Years now of those little pictures torn out of the ugly books I've made. It's the closest I come to getting a look at all those tremendous forces: all the things coming toward me, all the things going on inside. It's the closest I get to seeing the ocean and the table in the same place. The closest I get to anguish and light. The mystery, joy, and agony of those wild years and those bitter years are on those pages, and that is a comfort to me.

I look back on those illuminated tiles and see someone who is struggling upstream of pride and lies, captive to a monstrous gloom, a punishing impatience, and a scattered confusion, someone knocked around by his own wounded honor, sudden terror, pushed and pulled by how hurt, scared, and upset he is, and yet captive also to an unconquerable light. Somehow at this table still. In this ocean, and at this table. Held together by the feast right now. Receiving Him, staying with Him, working with Him by hearing, through prayer, and as an offering.

When I've made enough of those illuminated tiles of Scripture I glue them as a background on a canvas and with a big Sharpie I draw big, wounded hands reaching down. Christ giving Himself to us by this good news.

All words of Scripture adding up to His single Word, the gracious offer of Himself, reaching out for us again with this good news. This bread by which we see Him, this light by which He gives Himself to us. I draw big, wounded hands reaching down and splitting an ocean, so there's just enough solid ground. A place to sit in this ocean and at this table.

WHAT I KNOW NOW is that it is only good news that gives me back to God, myself, and others. It is only this solemn procession that leads me back to myself. It is only by the means of grace that I get to have a thing called myself.

This Simple Rhythm, this simple life, this long, slow walk with His Spirit, has been the only thing that has made it possible to claim this thing called myself, the only thing that has made it possible to stop flailing when I'm hurt, scared, and upset. To be quiet, simple, and gentle when I'm hurt, scared, and upset. To stop taking things back and making things right.

More than anything over these last five years what I have wanted was that ease: that thing called quiet, simple, and gentle in that place. What I wanted was a kind of repose, a kind of composure that I felt had been taken from me, that was no longer mine if the worst had happened and nothing made sense and everything had fallen apart. To have that stillness even when I was hurt, scared, and upset, even when I felt so crumbly, flickering, and helpless.

There was a kind of flailing I was doing, that I'd seen done, that I didn't want to do anymore. I wanted another way to be okay. I wanted the undeserved stillness I'd found in the auditorium, that I was finding in coffee shops, on Zoom calls, and in my sad, green truck. I wanted the stillness where you don't take things back and make things right. The stillness where you stop flailing. The stillness where you hear good news instead of flailing. The stillness where you sit at a table. The stillness where you keep a feast. I wanted to be quiet, simple, and gentle when I was hurt, scared, upset. To somehow just be hurt, scared, and upset. To be at ease even if I was ashamed, afraid, and in despair. To be quiet, simple, and gentle with just how bad it was.

That underserved stillness—that thing called quiet, simple, and gentle—was as close as I could get to the thing called myself. As close as I got to being at ease. The stillness of hearing this good news. The stillness of being rescued, led, and given.

I would have traded the world, every pleasure and possibility, to be at ease in this ocean of chaos and hard feelings. To be rescued, led, given, to be quiet, simple, and gentle even when I was hurt, scared, upset.

Because so often I was still just pacing the driveway of that Airbnb, restless, arguing with myself.

I spent five years in coffee shops and Zoom calls and my sad, green truck, learning I would only gradually be made quiet, simple, and gentle. And never on my own. Every day, multiple times a day, I had to be cleansed and presented. My trust had to be rescued so that I could be quiet, my attention had to be led so that I could be simple, and my intentions had to be given back to me so that I could be gentle.

I had to be cleansed and presented before I could be quiet, simple, and gentle.

Cleansed and presented. All at once by His dying and rising, and day by day as I heard this news and offered a more Ordinary Hospitality.

The Emmaus walk, this solemn procession, was a long walk toward that thing called quiet, simple, gentle. This slow walk out of pride and lies, through trouble and loss, toward meaning and rest. This slow walk we make with Christ. It made me feel like myself again. Myself again in coffee shops and a sad, green truck.

It was really my trust—was really mine again—but it had to be rescued by His gospel so that I could die with Christ who died. It was really my attention—was really mine again—but only if it was led by His gospel through His Spirit, so I could rise with the Christ who's risen. And they were really my intentions—they were really mine again—but only if my intention was to be given in His name, given by His gospel through His Spirit, given to His fellowship.

I was myself again, but only if I was at this feast. I was myself again but only as I was cleansed by this news and presented as this offering. And all through His Spirit, and all of it a mending. Unchanging news that continues to change us. Every day, multiple times a day. A thousand times a year. A million times in a lifetime.

That's the hardest thing to get back to after all you've lost, all the trouble you're in, all the lies you've been told, and with pride your only shepherd. The hardest thing to get back to is yourself. And I think only good news does it. Only good news gives us back to ourselves.

The hardest thing: to be yourself, to be quiet, simple, and gentle in this place. When our trust and attention are held captive and our truest intentions are lost to us. The hard thing is to be quiet, simple, and gentle with all we've lost, all the trouble we're in.

And so by this Simple Rhythm, this solemn procession, this simple good news, this good undertow, I was constantly being washed back toward myself, constantly refound, rethreaded, sewn back by His gospel, through His Spirit, to His fellowship. Constantly, constantly, constantly cleansed and presented by this good news.

Cleansed and presented so that I could be quiet, simple, and gentle. Quiet, simple, and gentle when I was hurt, scared, and upset. Quiet, simple, and gentle, when I was crumbly, weak, helpless.

Who knew I would feel myself to be made of such tender threads as trust, attention, and intention? The trust He rescues, the attention He leads? The intentions He gives back to us? Or that I must be rethreaded each day, multiple times a day?

That I would not really have myself back until I had the same kind of day? Until I was on this walk? Until I found the table in this place? Held together by the feast right now. Good news and the few strange signs this news is true.

It took a long time to feel like I even had those things back, or that they could ever come back—trust, attention, intentions. And even then, and often still, I still feel like my trust is a crying child, my attention a wild animal, my intentions a lost coin. That

I am crumbly, flickering, and helpless. That I may not really still be there under everything that happened to me.

I picture it now—that serpent, those waves, that undertow. And I draw the picture with that Sharpie, that picture where the hands of Christ are coming down, splitting the waves, so that a little table rests on a little bit of solid ground. There is bread and wine at the table, and an odder, kinder, gentler light casting its radiance from the table. And the table is there and I'm there, even as the serpent coils and the undertow pulls. And the great waves crash in, those great big hard feelings, and I see them and I'm crumbly, flickering, and helpless but I'm still there, and that table is still there. And I'm there and I'm cleansed and presented and I'm quiet, simple, and gentle. I'm still there even though I'm hurt, scared, and upset, and crumbly, flickering, and helpless. And I'm still there and I'm seeing that those waves don't get to have all of me. That I get to stand with those hard feelings, and feel the great waves of them, and they don't wash me away, and they don't get to have all my trust, attention, and intention.

On Fridays we sit and do that short liturgy before our sanctuary space called Open Hours. A short liturgy in a stuffy room. I hold out some of those ugly little books I've made myself. I give them to the crusty locals and a few volunteers. I try to give people the same kind of day. I try to lead the solemn procession.

I see my friend smoking outside with his smile and his sad eyes. My friend, the younger looking, long-haired Mister Rogers. My friend, a thin man in his late forties with a gentle smile, a sense of humor, and acute schizophrenia.

I ask him if he wants to join and he says yes. He comes upstairs with a few others and I put the ugly book in his hands. I've tried to make it simple. He likes that it does not change. Unchanging news that continues to change us. I just wish he understood those words, and I don't know if he does. He comes up and joins us.

It's hard to do a liturgy here above the sanctuary, here at this third space. There are always interruptions. People can't sit still. The noises outside, the noises nearby. I feel the impatience they feel. It feels like the serpent draws especially close, the waves get especially big. But somehow we keep going. Mumbling the words. Hearing good news. Reciting the promises of Scripture. Claiming safe passage. Counting on the means of grace. Finding the table in this place. Waiting for someone to come in and start yelling. Waiting for it to get too hot or for people to get too bored and for it to get too long. Waiting for the worst to happen. Waiting for everyone to get up and leave.

Waiting to be knocked overboard, knocked out by something, by anything. By someone getting bored and leaving, by someone coming in yelling.

I'm leading this simple liturgy. I feel like I'm out on a limb. I feel like the light might go out. That everything is rotten and foul. That too much has happened. That we've lost too much, that we're in too much trouble, that we've been told too many lies. We sit there, it seems like, at the end of the world.

It's easier in coffee shops, in my sad, green truck, on Zoom calls. There's control.

Doing this liturgy on Fridays, there's no control. Just exposure. It feels like there's just this ocean.

The crusty locals, my wounded soul, and I. This way to be together. This regard, this anguish and light. This place we meet.

"Is this stupid?" I've asked myself again and again. I hold out the tender, stubborn light of regard.

"No, it isn't."

"Then why do I feel like everything's going to fall apart?"

"Because it might."

"What do I do?"

"You keep sitting."

"For how long?"

"Until the bitter years are done."

"Where do I sit?" I ask.

"In this ocean, at this table."

My handsome friend with acute schizophrenia looks at me, ugly book in hand.

"What page are we on?" he says. He's peering down. He's interested. He's following along. I can't believe it.

I think he knows. He somehow knows. Even here, even with this liturgy. The reality of Christ, the forgiveness of sins, the homecoming offered only in Him.

This liturgy. This way to be together. This anguish and light. This place we meet.

This place we're supposed to be. To share in something, and see each other clearly. The joy we offer, the joy in offering. The One we share in when we share something like this.

ABUSED IN AN OFFICE. A vision in an auditorium. Mended in coffee shops and a sad, green truck.

Why do I sit in coffee shops and work through these long rhythms, liturgies, and songs? So I can be with people again. So I can give regard. The work I head to afterward—caregiving and chaplaining—is about being with people and giving them regard. Learning to be with people again. To offer those things by which Christ gathers a people to Himself.

The only shore I've found is other people. The only arrival I've found is the bitter feast of others, and the possibility of gentleness.

The same kind of day is the only thing that has helped me make beautiful things, that has led me to beautiful things. And the most beautiful thing to me is the place of rest. The most beautiful thing I offer is a more Ordinary Hospitality. To be with people in such a way that Christ is revealed and they are transfigured.

The same kind of day so I could be with people again. The same kind of day to turn me into the stained-glass window of wasted time. The same kind of day to sing that song, make that smudge, give off this stench: this world blurring to the world to come. Cleansed and presented so that I'm out with people again. A part-time chaplain.

Learning to give regard, keep company, and make a place of rest. Learning the fierce song of gentleness, grief, and gladness. The song by which He gathers a people to Himself. This Simple Rhythm: preparation for this obstinate grace, preparation for the mundane agonies of divine love. Preparation for the gift of regard.

To give regard, and be given in His name, and given to His joy. To see Him more clearly as we offer a more Ordinary Hospitality. Learning His gentleness, entering His grief, sharing His gladness.

A simple life with this good news. Good news that gives us back. To have ourselves back is to finally have ourselves to give. To finally serve the table in this place. To have arrived at the gentleness that is close at hand.

And I was glad for coffee shops and Zoom calls and my sad, green truck, glad for this one Groundhog Day, because for a long time in this wild country all I felt was that I was ruined. A big flailing mess. That I wasn't there under all the rubble of what happened to me.

For me, to feel ruined, to feel damned, to feel cursed, was to feel like you could not be gentle. Not a physical gentleness, but gentleness in approach, in speech, in tone and manner. To be ruined was to feel like I couldn't have a gentle tone, a gentle way.

To feel like I couldn't be gentle like my father. The man who soared over his ruined hips to reconcile with me.

To be thrashing in the ocean of chaos and hard feelings, to be flailing like that, is to feel like you are unable to be gentle with people as they are and the world as it is. You are stuck trying to take things back and make things right. You are stuck there and you are ruined and there is no way to be gentle.

It's a pain that cannot become sorrow. A pain that cannot become anguish and light. A pain that cannot become gentleness, grief, and gladness. A pain that can only become this flailing. A stranger to yourself and a god to others. A pain that cannot become regard.

And the opposite was true. To be gentle, to learn gentleness, was to finally be okay. That is what I wanted to know—that someone who'd been ruined can be quiet, simple, and gentle again. Could be okay even when they're hurt, scared, upset. Quiet, simple, and gentle with all they've lost and all the trouble they're in. That something could make me stop flailing.

I kept thinking I needed something other than good news.

Something more than a Simple Rhythm, a Crucified Heart, a more Ordinary Hospitality. Something other than the feast right now.

But what I've found—and here I can only speak for myself—is that gentleness is not a feeling, it is a gift, an intention given back to us by this means of grace. That this good news can even change what we want so that we want to be given in His name.

I've found that gentleness is an intention, a gift, a possibility given back to us by His gospel, through His Spirit, and in His fellowship.

A Simple Rhythm to lead me back to the gentleness close at hand. Good news that crucifies the heart. A gospel to deepen our trust, shepherd our attention, and give us back to each other. To give us back to the gentleness close at hand. To give us back to the regard we give.

To be ruined, to be gentle, and to finally be okay. To finally arrive at this stoop.

A FEW YEARS INTO THAT WILD COUNTRY, a few years after the abuse in the office, a few years into coffee shops and a sad, green truck, a young friend mailed us an invitation to his wedding. It was young man who was at church with me when I thought I was supposed to be a pastor. Back when I thought I was supposed to be *his* pastor. When I left, we'd stayed friends, and he saw—I thought—the best and worst of me at the time. The best and worst of a caregiver and part-time chaplain. The best and worst of someone who just wanted to stop flailing. He'd joined in the liturgies, joined in the hospitality. He'd moved away, met someone, was getting married. He wanted us there.

I got the invitation and started to cry. I was crying and looking at my wife, who saw that I was crying. Crying there, in my thinning hair and my big, relaxed clothes. Crying the only way you can when you are a part-time chaplain.

"It means we were good to him, right?" I said. "It means we did right by him? It means we were good to him, right?"

I wanted to know. Was I good to him? Was he better off for having known me? Was I still a gift to others? Even with all I'd lost, all the trouble I was in? Even though I was a failed pastor? Even though I barely even felt like myself?

"Yes, baby," she said. "It means you did right by him."

We'd given regard. We'd been gentle.

I was crying because when I look back on my life my only regret is not having treated people well. I've only regretted cruelty. I've only regretted disregard. I've only regretted what I would do to be okay.

The purpose of this rhythm was to sit in coffee shops and a sad, green truck and find another way to be okay. To be with Jesus and then to anoint and not devour. To be with Jesus and then to uphold and not destroy.

And if we were at his wedding then we had done that. We were some of the people there who had done that. We were some of the people who had treated him well.

If we were invited to his wedding then there was a simple life with this good news. There was such a thing as trust in Christ and regard for others. And if there was such a thing as trust in Christ and regard for others then it meant I wasn't ruined. And the rhythm, liturgy, and song, these books, gel pens, and harmonicas were my simple life with this good news, that made possible my trust in Christ and my regard for others.

I couldn't understand. The irony, the eeriness, the strangeness. My pastor and my denomination had given me these rhythms, liturgies, and songs. These things to hold on to. My mentor and my denomination had given me this Simple Rhythm. They taught me how to be with Jesus, and then they taught me how not to treat people.

They gave me a Simple Rhythm and then that complete disregard.

And I just didn't understand how people who loved these words could do these things. How can people eat this bread and see this light and offer this instead?

Wasn't this Simple Rhythm to be put to the greater service of treating people well? Wasn't it the job of this Simple Rhythm to prepare us for Ordinary Hospitality? This word about His Word, this radiance of His light, this song by which Christ gathers a people to Himself? Our most basic, tender, and visible sign that this news is true?

Didn't these rhythms, liturgies, and songs prepare us to go and see the crushed? Didn't they prepare us for the gentleness close at hand? To give regard? As kinda sorta chaplains? To prepare us for this regard? This sign of the cross? This share in His joy? This anguish and light? This place we meet? This most basic, tender, visible sign of the reality of Christ, the forgiveness of sins, and the homecoming offered only in Him?

WEREN'T THESE WORDS supposed to make us gentle?

A gentleness that was not a feeling or a reaction but a revelation? A refusal to take things back and make things right? A gift, a decision, an intention given back to us?

I was in the coffee shops and the sad, green truck to prepare myself for this gentleness, to prepare myself for the gift of regard. For being with people again.

This gentleness—a fierce intention, a firm decision, and a terrifying risk. And this regard—the gentleness close at hand. Given only in His name. The longing for Christ to be revealed to the ruined god, the frightened child, and the complete stranger. To be revealed to all of us. A tender, stubborn light held out to the world's wounded honor, the world's sudden terror, the world's unconquerable loathing. Our song to the world as it is and people as they are. Our sign that this news is true.

This possibility, this gift, this decision: the crucifixion of certainty and the end of defending yourself. The renunciation of manipulation. The end of refusal and defiance. The end of taking things back and making things right. The end of having to prove ourselves. The end of taking a swing at a world that has taken something from us. And yet not passivity and not avoidance, but simply being given. Simply giving regard, the sign of His gentleness.

And gentleness demands the same kind of day. It demands we be given back by good news. It demands the trust rescued by the gospel and the attention led through His Spirit. And it demands a feast right now. It demands a table in this place. It is only Word and Spirit that makes it possible to turn our face toward people. Only Word and Spirit that makes it possible to never turn our face away.

His gentleness making its demands, insisting on a Simple Rhythm, a more Crucified Heart, a more Ordinary Hospitality.

Because when you are gentle, and when you refuse to take things back and make things right, the waves get only bigger. When you refuse to take things back and make things right you *begin* to feel hurt, scared, upset. You *begin* to feel all you've lost and the trouble you're in. And to feel those things without the benefit of pride or lies is to grieve. To feel those things without retaliation or avoidance is to grieve. Gentleness gives birth to grief. A better kind of painful grieving. Trusting Him with the screaming loss of things.

That is why it is important to say that gentleness, to me, is not a feeling. I think it is better to call it a gift and a decision born of trust and attention. That is because gentleness never feels gentle. It often feels unacceptable, and the unacceptable is always felt as grief.

We grieve the loss of outcomes, we grieve the loss of who we thought we were and what we thought life would be like. We crash and burn on an idea of ourselves and grieve what we thought was going to happen. We grieve the unacceptable and the intolerable.

Grief is a willingness to feel that way. To hurt and lose and feel and still be gentle. Grief is trusting Christ with the screaming loss of things. Grief is giving regard to yourself and others. The impossible possibility: to be quiet, simple, and gentle when we're hurt, scared, and upset and feel crumbly, flickering, and helpless. To trust Him with the screaming loss of things. To feel this way and hear this news instead of taking things back and making things right. Regard is the gentleness close at hand, a gentleness that turns to grief as we turn ourselves toward the bitter feast of others.

This grief is not just pain. It is also a longing. A longing that waits for Christ to clothe our shame, for Christ to walk us through fear, for Christ to give us back meaning and rest. Grief is a longing that refuses to take things back or make things right but insists on waiting for Christ to be who He says He is. Grief is the joyful end of pride, lies, trouble, and loss. It is the bitter feast. And bitter feast is Christ as well. He is there whenever wounded, selfish people are given to wounded, selfish people.

And regard is the place where all that gentleness and grief happens. The place of anguish and light. The place where gentleness makes demands. The place where we sing that song by which Christ gathers a people to Himself.

This regard, this place, this gentleness close at hand, is the place where we grieve instead of taking things back and making things right. The place where we stand with the screaming loss of things. Regard is how we announce this feast.

Regard is the place we are transfigured, and where the world is changed by what we offer. The place of anguish and light. The place where we decide what we need to be okay. The place we are cleansed and mended as we are given by Christ to others. The place where we see Him more clearly. Learning His gentleness, entering His grief, sharing His gladness.

The phone call, the argument, the helping out, the difficult conversation. Regard is the place of gentleness and grief. The place of anguish and light. The place of unbearable tension and unbearable love. The place we meet.

Regard is the place of revelation, of picking up the phone or not picking up the phone, listening to a boring story or telling people we have to go. The place where we scream or don't scream. Where we lash out or don't. The place where we decide what this is all about.

Regard is the place we lose and feel the loss. And it's awful and it sucks and it's great and I'm not ready. I am not ready for the regard. I'm not ready to grieve, and I am not ready to lose.

Not ready for the tender, stubborn light of regard. For a better kind of grief, a more Ordinary Hospitality. The gentleness close at hand. The possibility of that gentleness.

And so Jesus is going to have to do it. He is going to have to give us back, to change what we even want.

Because there's nothing left but to share in who He is and what He's done. There's nothing left but who we are this table. There are only helpless sinners, honored guests, and humble servants.

It's a few years after I was crushed, abandoned, and alienated, and I'm talking to my parents on a Zoom call, going on and on and on and not even irritated because this is small talk and my parents gave me this gift of small talk. This place we meet, this way to be together. My dad's friendly banter. Absent-minded tenderness. The man who soared who over his broken hips to reconcile with me. And I found that the refusal was gone, that I could talk again, that I could talk again forever. And it was just this small talk.

The gentleness close at hand. This place we meet. This way to be together. This regard. This anguish and light. This sign of His cross. This share in His joy.

I see my father's face on Zoom. This man whose voice I heard one night in a dream. I still hear what he told me. In a world where the worst happens, and nothing makes sense and everything falls apart, he told me, "Be gentle, consistent, and never turn your face away."

I stand in the center of the sanctuary space while I get the coffee ready, the coffee that will vindicate this good news. I'm a wounded soul with my thinning hair, my big, relaxed clothes, making the coffee that will vindicate this good news. I'm there and my friend, the long-haired Mister Rogers, is there, and he's talking. I'm clearly busy and he's talking. I'm clearly busy, and clearly very needed elsewhere. There are clearly things that need me and my solutions. But he's there with his smile, and his sad eyes, and he's looking at me and firmly, gently telling me things. Things I can't really follow at all but all the while I know that if I move this moment will be gone and the goodness of it will be gone, the goodness of the thing itself is gone. If I leave now, we lose what we say by just being here, the Person we reveal by just being there. And I know this excruciating stillness is a loss, a grief, that somehow reveals Christ. I know this regard is anguish and light.

Regard doesn't save people, good news does. But regard is our most tender, basic, and visible sign that this news is true. That nothing that happens can change what life's about. It is the vindication of this good news.

Regard, the excruciating possibility, and the gentleness close at hand. The sign of His cross, our share in His joy. This anguish and light. This place we meet.

My friend talks, his hands moving, trying to explain what's in his head to me and neither of us sure what to make of it. And I stand there, resisting effectiveness, resisting everything except handing over my complete attention to my friend, this long-haired younger-looking Mister Rogers with acute schizophrenia, telling him with my gaze that I am his, that my time is his. Just being here, just being here. Saying the thing we say by just being here.

And I can feel it. I can feel myself crashing and burning my on an idea of myself, losing what I thought this day would be like, losing honor, security, and what I thought fulfillment would be like, to be out here with him too long. Just standing still while urgent things sweep by. A small moment set here instead of anywhere else. And I have to ask myself at that moment, what is this? What am I doing?

The light of Christ pouring in through the stained-glass window of wasted time. An offering that casts His light. An offering by which Christ gathers His people to His table.

I know that I'm singing to him, standing here, a wounded soul with my thinning hair and my big, relaxed clothes. I am singing the only song I know: the fierce song of gentleness, grief, and gladness.

Singing it to him by giving regard. Grieving, standing, singing, holding out the tender, stubborn light of regard. Holding it out to us both. This regard, this gentleness close at hand. This anguish and light. The sign of the table in this place.

Holding a light out to my crushed friend. Whose mind is not his friend. Just standing there: the only way I know to tell him about the table in this place. This place where the worst happens and nothing makes sense and everything falls apart.

My friend, a younger-looking, long-haired Mister Rogers.

My friend, a thin man in his late forties with a gentle smile, a sense of humor, and acute schizophrenia.

REGARD: THE GENTLENESS CLOSE AT HAND. Regard: a gentleness that gives birth to grief and gladness. Because that is what I know I want. That is the thing to want most: gladness.

The only safe passage in this place of pride and lies, trouble and loss, chaos and disaster: to see Him more clearly, to want only this deep gladness.

I am a part-time chaplain. And I chose this life for one reason: for the goodness of it, the deep gladness of it.

Five years into this wild country I went home to see my parents. I went home to see my Grandma. It's sad—she's too old and frail to live alone, so she's with my parents now. She sits in my old room, my childhood room. She sits there amongst my books. My childhood room is like a nursing home now. It has her special bed, full of things she needs.

She walks around the house sometimes, and visits downstairs, but she mostly sits in the room a lot, and watches Westerns with the nursing aide sitting with her. It never dawned on me to join her, to sit with her there, to watch Westerns. It never dawned on me that that would have meaning.

What I had felt toward that room was a reluctance to go in. A withdrawal. I was a complete stranger to my childhood room. A childhood that had once had all my gladness and now was a sign of something else. A sign of decline, of getting older. I don't know. Maybe just a sign of the end. A sign of things falling apart.

But working on this book, and wondering why I sit on stoops, and finding this same kind of day and the gentleness close at hand, I felt led to go in there and to give regard and be good company.

And I sat with her, her healthcare supplies mixed in with my childhood books, and realized the gladness was still there. I realized there is nothing past good company. Good company is its own light. The goodness of the thing itself. An offering doesn't have to be anything else because it is its own sign, and it strikes its own deep note of rest. It is its own radiance of that feast. Its own word about the Word. Its own song about a table.

I'd like to think I did it to be nice, but I didn't. I did it for the deep gladness of it. To give regard, and be given in His name, and to see Him more clearly as we give a more Ordinary Hospitality.

The deep gladness of seeing Him more clearly. A gladness I would follow into the depths of hell if it meant I could be a part of it. An honored guest at the very heart of things.

How did I miss it? This joy we offer, this joy in offering. The gentleness close at hand.

Why would I sit on the stoop with old men? Why was I just sitting there with my Granny? For the deep gladness of it. The deep gladness of the thing itself.

I'd forgotten all about it. And the Lord has asked me to serve His table, and to go see the crushed, so I would know, so that I wouldn't forget. So that I would remember the deep gladness.

The deep gladness of the thing itself. This way to be together. This place we're supposed to be. This place we meet. To share in something, and see each other clearly. The joy we offer, the joy in offering. The gentleness close at hand. The One we share in when we share something. A life in Christ that includes me seeing her, her seeing me.

It had been a long time since we'd sat together like this, gently swaying in front of Westerns. I'd needed so much time in coffee shops and a sad, green truck. So many days in mercy's solemn procession. This long, slow walk to the gentleness close at hand. This joy we offer, the joy in offering.

To be here now. To arrive at this place. This place we meet.

Abused in an office. A vision in an auditorium. Mended in coffee shops and a sad, green truck. And here: on the stoop at Grandma's house.

And I remembered now the gladness I'd always known. Why did it take so long to get back to feeling like myself again? To get back to what I already knew?

Things like this:

Being an older child—ten or eleven—and taking an hour to push little kids I didn't know on a swing because they asked me to. I knew I was supposed to push them on that tire swing, and that if I stopped pushing them there would be no one to push them. I knew that if I stood there pushing them they would have fun, this kind of fun, a kind of fun they weren't used to. And so I pushed them. It was the goodness of it, that's what it was—the goodness of it, the gladness of it. The goodness of the thing itself. This way to be together.

Things like this:

Being in a van full of loud children. All the kids were screaming. And the mother who wasn't my mother but was the mother of some of the other kids was about to cry. I could sense she was about to cry. She said the kid who was the quietest would get an ice cream cone. And I was the quietest, but I didn't even want ice cream. What I wanted was what was happening to her, the day, this moment, to not be so hard. I wanted that for her and so I was quiet. And it was for the goodness of the thing itself. This brighter light, this darker shade of blue, this deeper note of rest.

Things like this:

My mom cooking burgers when I was ten years old. We ate in the living room and by the time she got there everyone had eaten and left and it made me sad that everyone ate and left and so I stayed. Just, I think, for the goodness of staying. The goodness of the thing itself. This way to be together. This brighter light, this darker shade of blue, this deeper note of rest. This place we're supposed to be. Things like this:

Being at a high school football game and seeing my brother come off the field after a sack or sittng there and talking with a waterboy no one liked. I found out they were talking about a video game they both liked. My brother was a superstar and this kid was a nobody. My brother in his big hulking football pads and the waterboy in his mousy V-neck just holding water and my brother leaning in to hear him a little better. I remember seeing that in the stands and thinking that that was the bravest, most beautiful thing I had ever seen. More beautiful than a beautiful face. More beautiful than beautiful music. I remember thinking the only beautiful thing was being good to people. I remember the deep gladness of it. I remember thinking of the goodness of the thing itself. This way to be together. This brighter light, this darker shade of blue, this deeper note of rest. This place we're supposed to be.

I remember thinking that the best, most beautiful thing in the world must be treating people well, and the worst and saddest thing in the world would be to not be able to treat people well. To not be able to be gentle. And to have no way to find the gentleness close at hand. This joy we offer, this joy in offering. The gentleness close at hand.

Things like this:

Being in college and befriending someone on the spectrum. He was difficult and loud. And I remember he would come into the cafeteria and look around nervously because everything was crowded and he didn't know where he was going to sit, and he would turn his head and see us and finally look like himself, cheery, cherubic. When he saw us, and knew he would have somewhere to be, he finally looked like who he was. And seeing him relax, seeing that he felt safe and was himself again, felt like the most noble and beautiful thing to give someone. To give people back to themselves for the goodness of it. The goodness of the thing itself. This way to be together. This brighter light, this darker shade of blue, this deeper note of rest. When there's nothing but who we are at His table. Nothing but helpless sinners, honored guests, humble servants. Nothing left but the offer of bread and the shining of light. To go do this and share in Christ together.

Things like this:

Working at a special needs camp and feeding a young quadriplegic his lunch. His wheelchair parked in the shade. I remember a lot of things were wrong with him medically and he couldn't talk anymore. I remember telling him a joke, telling him about my dog, and his whole chair shaking with a laughter I had not expected and could not have predicted. I remember how his laughter defeated everything, the sadness of his life and the sadness of mine. I remember understanding this was joy. The thrill of meaning. The possibility of heading somewhere. A special kind of being given. I remember the gladness. The goodness of time and laughter. The goodness of the thing itself. I remember feeling like I had arrived somewhere. That everything was worth it if it meant being here with him and this getting to happen.

The goodness of the thing itself. This way to be together. This brighter light, this darker shade of blue, this deeper note of rest. This place we're supposed to be. When there's nothing but who we are at His table. Nothing but helpless sinners, honored guests, humble servants. Nothing but the offer of bread, the shining of light.

I remember that the most important thing, the most beautiful thing, was getting to be here with him. I remember that being there, getting to be there, felt like what this was all about. This way to be together. This place we're supposed to be. To share in something, and to see each other clearly. The One we share in when we share anything. This place we're supposed to be.

It felt like I knew what I was for. It felt like I was real because I knew what I was for. It felt like everything added up to getting to be with other people again. This way to be together. An honored guest at the very heart of things.

Why was I asked to serve this table? Why was I a part-time chaplain?

To sit with old men. To sit with my granny. To remember. To remember.

I GO HOME and see my granny.

And I remember. And I come back here, to this work, to all these wounded, lovely, selfish people, and sit with them. To arrive on this stoop. My granny helped me arrive on this stoop.

I go see a friend who's losing parts of his foot. Nothing to say to him other than what I say with my physical body. The stench of Christ. The incarnate funk of just being here. Nothing to be but there, nothing to be but a sign of the Person this is all about. A sign that nothing that happens can change what life's about. What have I arrived at? Only at this stoop. Only at the thing we say by being here. Only at being given.

I go to the care home by our church, where people live who can't live by themselves. An older man there, a friend, comes up to me. The man who had the boom box.

He comes up to me and says, "You came here just to see us, didn't you?"

"Yeah," I say. "Just to see you." For the goodness of the thing itself. This way to be together.

And I remember thinking that the best thing has to be just being here. To be able to be here with them. That has to be the best thing. The goodness of the thing itself.

I remember thinking that this world is not enough. Nothing here is enough. But it is enough to be given. It is more than enough to be a sign of the table in this place.

I go and see the crushed. And I chose this life because of the goodness of it, the gladness of it. I'm a part-time evangelist and kinda sorta chaplain so I can remember the gladness of it.

Knowing that my truest intention, my deepest longing, was to be given. And my trust and my intentions can always be given back to me. Cleansed by this news, presented as this offering. And all through His Spirit and all of it a mending.

I've found myself crying these five years in this wild country, the place where the worst happens and nothing makes sense and everything falls apart. Five years in coffee shops and a sad, green truck.

With the serpent close, the waves big, the undertow strong, I cry. At coffee shops I cry. With my thinning hair, my big, relaxed clothes, I cry. I cry hoping I have not missed out on goodness. The sweet cry for mercy.

5

AN ORDINARY HOSPITALITY

Another word for the regard we give,
the company we keep, and
the places of rest we make

I BELIEVE IN THE GIFT OF REGARD, a more Ordinary Hospitality. One of the few good things that are not lies. I believe in regard, company, and places of rest. I believe they are the gentleness close at hand. I believe this gentleness is a word about that Word, that Word of cleansing, provision, and rest. An invitation to a table. The radiance of a feast. Our most basic, tender, and visible sign that this news is true. That regard is a gentleness that becomes grief and gladness. The strangest sign of Christ Himself.

I believe that without regard nothing is beautiful and nothing is good. That without regard even good things hurt. Without regard a free meal and free clothes and necessary help are an assault, a provocation, and an insult. And if there is something I don't understand it's the decision we've made to give Christ to the world without giving regard.

I believe that this regard, this gentleness close at hand, involves a loss. Regard will make us hurt, scared, and upset. It involves a loss of honor, security, and purpose. Gentleness is the end of taking things back, making things right, and proving ourselves. It is our most painful gift, a fierce intention, an obstinate grace only made possible by good news that crucifies the heart and prepares us for an Ordinary Hospitality.

I believe regard is wasted time. It is a loss that reveals Christ. A loss that is also His radiance, the radiance of His light, the strangest sign of Him.

I believe the gift of regard is the smallest of seeds. It seems trivial—as trivial as donuts and coffee and Uno cards. But I believe it carries, hidden in the gesture, the same bread and light of His dying and His forgiveness. It is sign that this news is true. It is a gift to the world as it is and to people as they are. It demands nothing of the world. Its only thought is that Christ might be revealed by it. A word about a Word. A song about a feast, to a world starved for some sign of Him.

I believe we go out into the world with this sign of Him. We don't invite people into it. We go out into the world with it. We go out into the world with an Ordinary Hospitality.

I believe in the gift of regard, and I believe in what that regard becomes: company and places of rest. Not by some tactic or strategy but by the inevitability of the gospel itself. The inevitability of good news that crucifies the heart and prepares us for an Ordinary Hospitality.

I believe that regard, company, and places of rest are such baffling gifts that they demand that Christ Himself work with us by His Word and Spirit for the building of His fellowship. These awful, baffling gifts demand the supernatural grace of the Holy Spirit, who makes it possible to believe in the gospel and somehow live as if it were true, who demands not that we simply give ourselves (which is not possible) but that we be given by Christ to others (which eventually becomes possible).

Five years in this place of pride and lies, trouble and loss, chaos and disaster. Out here with the crushed. Out here where we get crushed by what life's like, and I look back on what I've seen. I've seen and known the Look of Those Transfigured by regard, company, and places of rest. The look of those changed by obstinate grace, our most tender, basic, and visible sign that this news is true. And I've seen and known the look of those disfigured and misshapen by the absence of regard, company, and places of rest.

I find myself allergic to the idea that there might be something more important than being good to people, something more important than the gift of regard, something more important than the gentleness close at hand. I find it a kind of blasphemy, a violation of the sacred. It is our sacred task to give regard, to never turn our face away.

Regard is the only answer I've found to the question I've had to ask—is there a beautiful, vigorous way to be in the world that involves neither avoidance, coercion, manipulation, or refusal? Can we make something beautiful without the hardness of our own hearts? Can we make something beautiful with only that stillness? Can we be quiet, simple, and gentle in this place and still make something beautiful?

I think we can, but the only thing I've found is the gift of regard. I've only found the gentleness close at hand. I've only found myself offering this. An offering that neither backs down nor charges ahead nor hurries to fix. An offering that simply turns its face to the world in gentleness, grief, and gladness.

But we have withheld the gift of regard. We have refused to turn our face to a world that is hurting, staggering under losses too great to bear without some sign of the reality of Christ, the forgiveness of sins, the homecoming offered only in Him. To a world that has lost all words, we have withheld these quiet signs of Christ, our quiet sign that this news is true.

We have withheld regard. We have refused to keep the world company. We have refused it any sign of rest. We have refused our most basic, tender, and visible signs of the reality of Christ, the forgiveness of sins, and the homecoming offered only in Him, and offered it only to those who have already made their return to the preached Word and the Lord's Supper in the fellowship of believers. We have refused to serve the world as it is. We have refused to pour out those costly graces available to us by Word and Spirit. To bless the world rather than curse it. To sing to the ruined god, the frightened child, the complete stranger. To offer the world the inheritance unique to us—this grief and gladness, this gentleness close at hand. We have decided we have nothing to give them. We have decided to not announce this feast. We have not let good news run its course. We have not let it take us anywhere. We have not let it crucify our hearts and prepare us for a more Ordinary Hospitality.

And I find myself grieving—grieving it in what I see, grieving it in myself. Wanting to say, "No, this is not our song. No, no, no. We have a better song than this. We have a gentler way to let everyone know this news is true."

We have good news that crucifies the heart and prepares us for a more Ordinary Hospitality. We can be cleansed by this news and presented as this offering. And all through His Spirit and all of it a mending. We have a long, slow walk with this His Spirit, the one who makes it possible to believe this news and somehow live as if it were true. We have a long, slow walk to the gentleness close at hand.

We don't have to agree with the world, but we must always sing to it. Even our opposition must hide a deeper friendship, our fierce longing for its good, to see the crushed upheld, this world transfigured by the revelation of Christ. To offer those things that reveal Him, that cast His light. These few, small signs that this news is true.

I SIT IN MY SAD, GREEN TRUCK. I sit with the twin gifts offered by my pastor and my denomination: a Simple Rhythm and complete disregard. The gift of devotion and the gift of neglect.

They showed me what life's about and what life's like. The table and the ocean.

How to make a gift of both?

My pastor and my denomination taught me how to be with Jesus and then introduced me to that place where the worst happens and nothing makes sense and everything falls apart.

That crushing became, in a way I'm still learning, an ordination. I cannot escape that I'm here to offer what I wasn't offered.

The crushing—transfigured only by Christ—has become a vocation. To go and see the crushed, to go and see the people the worst has happened to. To go out into this place, to go out to where the worst happens and nothing makes sense and everything falls apart. To go out there and offer this most basic, tender, and visible sign that this news is true.

How to say it? How to say it and mean it? Why has it taken so long to say it and mean it? Why has it taken so long for all that trouble and loss to become this sorrow, for this sorrow to become a longing, for this longing to become a joy, a gladness, a vocation?

What can our loss hope to become if not sorrow, longing, and joy? What can our pain hope to become if not gentleness, grief, and gladness? And who but Christ can turn all that loss into anything else—into anything at all? What does it mean to say that He even wants our losses?

I have a cross hung up on my rearview mirror. It's made out of the rebar they put in concrete. When the concrete's busted up the old rebar shows. When the rebar is exposed, it works loose. When it works loose pieces of it get scattered. Some of those scattered pieces look like a cross. I picked one up, a block down from the stoop, and used some of the thread I use for my ugly little books to make an impromptu necklace for myself. It hangs in the rearview mirror of this sad, green truck I go see people in. The truck that takes me to where I'll go to give regard, as a part-time chaplain.

I wear it as I get out of the truck and head toward the stoop, toward the bitter feast of the others. The gentleness close at hand. Knowing, somehow, that the bitter feast is Christ as well. That the anguish is light, and the sorrow is gladness.

There are folks there already. The crusty locals abide. This cross hanging down my big, relaxed clothes. A ragged sign of the cross that is His joy, because His joy is to have His people back. This cross hanging down my neck, my neck holding out my face, my face turning to them. My face turning to them in regard, this regard the sign of His cross. This anguish and light. This place we meet.

What is the cross if not His song to us? A song to gather us to His table?

I take the cross with me, to where I'm going and to who I'm going to see. To the people I'm waiting on. Waiting for what they want to say and if they want to say it.

I take it with me, put it in my shirt pocket or hang it around my neck as a reminder to not be an ass. A reminder that there is nothing to take back and make right. A reminder that there is only the gentleness close at hand.

Taking that ugly cross on my long, slow walk. The only thing I can do with a wounded soul, thinning hair, and my big, relaxed clothes. Limping on down to see folks. Limping toward this wasted time. Toward the most basic, tender, and visible sign that this news is true. This brighter light, this darker shade of blue, this deeper note of rest.

"I HEAR YOU TALK TO PEOPLE NO ONE WANTS." Someone once said that to me at the coffee shop I trust Jesus at, before I get in my sad, green truck, play the harmonica, jump on the Zoom call, put the ugly ol' cross on and become a part-time evangelist and kinda sorta chaplain, with my thinning hair and my big, relaxed clothes. The things that make me feel like myself.

I've thought of worse summaries of what I do. I thought, yes, that's what I do, that's part of what I do. I go to sad places where the worst has already happened: care homes, psych wards, downtown sidewalks.

This is where His dying and rising have taken me, this is where rhythm, patience, and longing have taken me. What it means to be cleansed by this news and presented as an offering. It means going out, out, out. Out to where the world has already ended. On this long, slow walk out to see the crushed, the folks I love, the wounded, selfish people the worst has happened to. A long, slow walk to the gentleness close at hand. Out to give regard. Regard: the table at the end of the world.

During Covid, when I first started this job, I lived twenty minutes from a care facility for the poor and mentally and physically disabled. It was a place I used to visit, and there were people in there I loved and tried to see when I could. Covid tore through there like the plague it was.

I'd heard a friend of mine was there—either dying or dead of Covid. A friend I'd known for years. Now he was there and dying and I couldn't see him. I couldn't explain why, but I just knew I was going to go down there and do what I could to see a person I couldn't see. To make a table at the end of the world, a sign of rest big enough for him to see outside his window while he died.

I bought sixty fake candle lights from Dollar Tree. I took them to the lawn outside the care facility, where the death rate from Covid was said to be 50 percent and where I heard my friend was dying. We made the ugly shape of a cross on the lawn with a crooked span of cheap lights. It felt like the first of my dumb tries, my first attempt at a song. My first stand against complete despair. My first try at the tender, stubborn light of regard. A basic, tender, visible sign that that this news is true.

I bought some cheap little electric lights. A bunch of them. Cheap lights to vindicate this good news. We put them on the lawn out by the care home, not sure whether the police would be called thinking we were staging a protest. We put those lights out on the lawn in the shape of a cross.

My hope was that someone who was dying could look out the window and see those few cheap lights in the shape of a cross. I hoped they would know from those few cheap lights that it mattered to us they were dying. If they were Christians I wanted them to know that other people were there as witnesses that they were dying as Christians. My hope was that out the window, people might look out as they were dying, and that they might live and die as Christians. I wanted to say, "You may be dying, but you do not belong to death." I wanted them to know they had safe passage. They still had a promise.

I wanted them to know there was still this sign. This place we meet, this place we're supposed to be. Even if it was this big dumb try.

A dark beyond dark. With those cheap lights only a gesture, only this tender, stubborn light of regard. Only this little thing that could be done. A word about the Word. A sign this news is true. A part-time evangelist, kinda sorta chaplain. A tender, stubborn light in a dark, hard place.

When we have a self to give, we give ourselves. We hold out this tender, stubborn light even when we're hurt, scared, and upset, even though we feel so crumbly, flickering, and helpless. We hold it out in this place where the worst happens and nothing makes sense and everything falls apart. We hold it out even though it always feels like it can be blown out. A fragile kind of radiance. The table at the end the world.

On that lawn I saw and see now the radical limit of that tender, stubborn light of regard. Only a sign. Only an offering. I saw the radical limit of regard, the radical ask of regard. The radical limit is we only have ourselves to give, only the gentleness close at hand, only this regard, only this company. To go out and see the people crushed by what life is like and sing to them the only song I know about what life's still about.

The radical ask is who we've been asked to sing to, who we've been asked to give ourselves to. We've been asked to offer it to the ruined god, the frightened child, the complete stranger. We've been asked to offer it out here, where the worst happens and nothing makes sense and everything falls apart. A tender, stubborn light. And the further out, the fiercer the song, the gentler the light.

"This gift, this offer, this regard," I thought when I was setting out those lights. "Is it really great or is it really dumb?"

Later I would ask, "Is it really great or really dumb to play Uno? To listen to Loretta Lynn? To sit on this stoop?"

Does it reveal who Christ is or how dumb we are? What does it mean that we can't fix even one thing here? That we can only visit? That we only have the gentleness close at hand? This anguish and light? This grief and gladness?

What was this moment, out here on this lawn? It was my first big dumb try. As a part-time evangelist and a kinda sorta chaplain. The first of all my big dumb tries.

A big dumb try. A parade of cheap lights on a lawn outside a care home full of people dying from Covid-19.

THAT EXPERIENCE TAUGHT ME A LOT. What is good news in a sad place where there's no way to make things right? What does it mean to visit people who aren't going to get better?

Perhaps at the time I was still focused on being a pastor again, on being taken seriously again. I was still focused on being effective. But if there's one thing I know the Lord wanted, it was for me to learn to be with people again, and to be with myself again. To be with people again, without avoidance or manipulation, without attack or refusal, without fixing or neglect.

And nothing made it clearer what it would mean to simply be with people than the care home. Where there's zero privacy, and the folks have little to no understanding or ability to understand. Where's there's no real way to make things better or make things right, and there's no church to get them to because they can't leave. Where they're stacked into a room and there's barely room to be human.

I take my collapsible stool that's supposed to be for fishing and plop myself down there. Where the only option is the gentleness close at hand. Where the only option is to partake of the incarnate funk of just being there, offering this quiet sign of Him. There with the tender, stubborn light of regard.

I think of the way that moment taught me how to be a part-time evangelist and kinda sorta chaplain in this place. How I learned to just go down to the place where the worst happens and nothing makes sense and everything falls apart. To limp on down to see folks. Limping on down to care homes, psych wards, downtown sidewalks.

Down to where our effectiveness is ineffective. Down to where there's no such thing as a career, no such thing as a successful ministry. Down to where there's only the gentleness close at hand. Visiting people who won't get better.

I live close to where I work, and I work in a town that could be described as poor. There are lots of folks in addiction, lots of mentally ill neighbors walking around somewhat aimlessly. Lots of people not doing well. But when I talk about going out to see the crushed, I'm not talking about any type of place, any specific geography or class.

I visit psych wards, care homes, and sidewalks in a small town. But the ocean isn't necessarily those places. The ocean is just what life is like. The table is just what life is actually about. Life itself, to me, is the place where the worst happens and nothing makes sense and everything falls apart. And I often have to remind myself that I was introduced to the worst that can happen and nothing making sense and everything falling apart by my pastor. He was the one who introduced me to this place.

And this happened to me in a nice office in the suburbs. Because this place is everywhere.

My thoughts about working in a place that might be described as poor are just this: In places like that there's less buffer between you and the worst that can happen, and little recourse when it does. You're more exposed.

But if you were to ask me what felt safer, a church or a run-down care home, a church or a stoop, a church or downtown bus stop, the choice is easy: the stoop.

It's easier to be out here. Out here where you don't have to trust a pastor, out here where you don't have to expect people to do the right things. Out here where there's no pretense that things are okay. Out here where you don't have to trust people all that much, where you can simply offer yourself to the world as it is and to people as they are.

I was just supposed to be there. I was just supposed to go downtown where people were and be with people who'd been crushed by what life's like. I was supposed to go down there, with my thinning hair, my big, relaxed clothes, and my big lumbering steps, and with the gentleness close at hand. Our most basic, tender, and vulnerable sign of the reality of Christ, the forgiveness of sins, and the homecoming offered only in Him.

The gentleness close at hand: my big dumb try. The gentleness Christ won for me at coffee shops and in a sad, green truck and on Zoom calls.

When I first started this job I would walk down to those care homes, I remember that. I'd get out of my sad, green truck and walk half an hour downtown. A wounded soul with big lumbering steps in my big, relaxed clothes, limping on down to care homes, psych wards, downtown sidewalks. I would walk downtown and sit with people, and that was all it seemed like there was to do. I felt too wounded to do anything else. Just sitting with them was its own arrival.

Good news that crucifies the heart and prepares us for a more Ordinary Hospitality. Cleansed and presented at the bitter feast of others. Presented to the crushed. Presented to the gentleness close at hand. Presented to a more Ordinary Hospitality.

Limping on down to see folks. Waiting for what they want to say and if they want to say it. All the suffering you find, all the problems, all the chaos in their life, all the things they've been made to feel—it feels like too much. A serpent that close, the waves that big. Calamity and disaster are always around. Shame, fear, and despair never stop crashing in. All the chaos and hard feelings just feel like darkness. Sometimes it's like the darkness is a force, a great swallowing maw. The unbearable strain, the dead end, the rising tide, the irresistible curse.

All too much. You sit at coffee shops and limp on down to care homes and just sit there. You sit there and wait for what they want to say and if they want to say it. You wait for the words they don't have. Words for all the things coming toward them and all the things going on inside them.

You see suffering, and you can't even take responsibility for it. It must be that some other reality is held responsible. You find that other people's problems are too much. Their illness, their grievances are too much. Their situation is unbearable, impossible. Their problems are too much, their illnesses too much, their shame, fear, and despair are too much. When it's not right and there's no way to make it right. Their behavior is unacceptable. It must be that only the broken body of a crucified Savior can be held accountable for these losses. It must be that only a feast can make it right.

Out here at care homes, out here where the lines are made clear, out here where there's no way to make it right. Nothing left but to share in who He is and what He's done. When there's nothing but who we are at His table. To go do this and share in Christ together. The One we share in when we share in something like this.

On this long, slow walk out of pride and lies, through trouble and loss, toward meaning and rest. This long, slow walk they take with Christ as their companion and you and me as a sign of His company.

But only a word about that Word. Only a sign this news is true. You are only there to give regard to them. You are there to say, "Your life is too much, your problems are too much, but you are not. You are here, and I give you my regard. That is what I give."

When all there is is darkness, all you have is the tender, stubborn light of regard. The gift of regard, a table at the end of the world.

Part-time evangelist, kinda sorta chaplain. With a fanny pack and stupid little ugly books. A Simple Rhythm to make it possible to give regard. Good news coming to me in rhythm, liturgy, and song, to deepen my trust in Him, shepherd my attention, and give others in His name. Good news to crucify the heart and prepare us for an Ordinary Hospitality. Good news to bind me closer to Him and closer to others.

I just never thought the flame would be so small. Such a narrow, rickety table. A song so slow and sad and quiet. Such a gentle note. That a brighter light could be such a dark shade of blue. I never thought I'd have to carry it where I carried it, or that it would be a flame that never went out. This regard. This sign of His cross. This anguish and light. This place we meet.

A light so small, and yet it does not go out. We are cleansed by this news and presented as this offering. And all through His Spirit: the one who makes it possible to believe in the gospel and somehow live as if it was true. And when you finally realize regard is a light that won't go out, you begin to ask: How far do you carry a light that won't go out?

I LIMP ON DOWN TO THE CARE HOME to give this regard. That is all it seems like there is, the giving of it. I've only found very ordinary things that can be done at the gates of hell. Only small tables at the end of the world.

I walk by the folks staring into walls, and I think again, "There is something worse than being in a place like this. There is something worse than being in hell. It's when it doesn't matter that you're here. It's when it doesn't matter to you or anyone else."

For the last few years I've known to go to places like this, and to not go for a long time without going to places like this. I knew I was too wounded to do much else. There's often other places I'd like to be, and I can always find a reason to not go. But when I'm paying attention to Scripture, and making the attempt of prayer, I always end up here. Good news dumps me out here. I don't know how I knew to go here. It's just where I knew to go.

This is where his dying and rising takes me: out to psych wards. Abused in an office. Mended in coffee shops and a sad, green truck. Limping toward care homes, psych wards, and downtown sidewalks.

Care homes. This rhythm left me here. Good news brings me here. The same kind of day brings me here. Cleansed and presented until I was headed toward care homes.

I've been at it these last five years, part-time evangelist, kinda sorta chaplain, and these are still the places I go, where my longings still take me. Where good news leaves me. Limping toward care homes, the bleak gray parts of life take on that darker shade of blue, that deeper note of rest.

Where all sad Grandmas go. Where no one gets better. People drifting around in scooters and wheelchairs looking like a bomb went off twenty years ago and they never figured anything out after that. It gets so easy to forget people are living and dying in a place like that.

Just go. Just go, just go, just go. The only thing He said, the only thing I know, to go there. To go with sorrow and longing. In gentleness, grief, and gladness. The joy we offer, the joy in offering. We carry Him with our longings, and with our longings He carries us. Out, out, out. To sing this song. The further out, the fiercer the song, the gentler the light. To go do this and share in Christ together.

I GO TO SEE ANOTHER PERSON in the care facility. We walk together and he tells me he hasn't been sleeping well. We get a soda and we walk to a bench in the parking lot by some trees. We sit in the same spot unless it's cold. He's allowed to walk out there with me. He has proven to them he will not try to escape. We listen to '80s pop and watch wrestling videos on my phone. He doesn't have his own.

I didn't know what to do when I first started visiting him. The only thing I knew to say was what my dad always said to me: "How 'bout a cake and a Coke?" Small talk and a snack.

He likes ginger ale, '80s pop, wrestling. Small talk has meant everything for us. This small talk, the gentleness close at hand. This way to be together. To share in something and see each other clearly. A life in Christ that includes me seeing him, him seeing me. Me trying to see what he's trying to show me, me trying to hold what he's trying to give. He knows Jesus and calls me his pastor, but can't get much past that without getting restless, upset, and angry that he can't understand. So we don't try to understand. We just sit there. The light of Christ pouring through the stained-glass window of wasted time. The only thing I have that reveals Him: all this wasted time. The willingness to lose the time we thought was ours. The joy we offer, the joy in offering. The deep gladness of a wounded, selfish person given to wounded, selfish people.

I go to see another friend on another floor. To take him out for a cigarette, to let his smoke drift on my new clothes. To wait for what he wants to say, and whether he wants to say it. To listen to him say the same things again and again until it's time to go.

I go to see another friend, in that same place. To play chess, to share his hot wings he wants me to try. He holds them out to me, and I take them and eat. To take the chicken wings offered to us. The gentleness close at hand. The joy we offer, the joy in offering. To learn how to be with people again.

He's the friend I thought was dead. He later told me he did die, but they brought him back to life with a defibrillator. He's good and alive but after that I started to not be able to understand him at all. I hold the things he shows me, but I can't understand what he's saying. It's just me holding things he puts in my hands. That's all we have now.

Sit where people sit, be where people are, eat what they're eating, look at what they show you. Always, always look at what they show you. Be gentle, consistent, and never turn your face away.

I've been able to do this: hot wings, wrestling videos. Benches and cigarettes. To be quiet, simple, and gentle in this place. Because I didn't have a career as a pastor, because the only thing left was the gentleness close at hand. The only thing left when the worst happens, nothing make sense, and everything falls apart. The only thing left is who we are at this table.

Because there is still this song. Still this regard, company, and sign of rest. When we're hurt, scared, and upset, when we feel crumbly, flickering, and helpless, there is still this song.

I think of seeing my friends here. I think of the time I'll spend seeing them, enjoying them, in eternity. I think of how I can even do it now, even in this sad place.

Going to see my friends here, that odder, kinder, gentler light all around. At times my friends look like that handsome, long-haired Mister Rogers. The look of those upheld by the feast right now. When ruined gods, frightened children, and complete strangers are cleansed and presented and become themselves again, even for just a little while. The look of a bunch of honored guests, even for just a little while. Even if it's just because of this regard, the regard I give, the regard I receive.

Every visit announces something. Every visit is the sign that this news is true. I see them now. I see their smile and their sad eyes at that table. Looking changed. Looking even more like themselves. I take their hot wings and see it even now.

LIMPING ON DOWN TO CARE HOMES. Learning to be with people again. Learning how to be with people who are hurt, scared, upset. How to be with them when I'm hurt, scared, and upset. Ruined gods, frightened children, complete strangers. I keep looking around but there is no other kind of person. There is no one else to reveal Christ to.

It is easier to go to care homes and psych wards. There's a sense of resignation. It is harder to limp down to the downtown sidewalks. You see people flirting with rock bottom and not quite there. And you wait for what they want to say and if they want to say it, and it is often more intense.

Their chaos and hard feelings awaken yours. Their flailing makes you want to flail. It's your life you're made to feel. The serpent that close, the waves that big, the undertow that strong, and you feeling so crumbly, flickering, helpless.

I sit down on a bench on a downtown sidewalk and I want to cry because there's no way to make it right. There's only good news right now. Good news that crucifies the heart and prepares us for an Ordinary Hospitality. There's only a simple life with this good news, that long, slow walk with His Spirit. There's only the feast right now. Only a few things to still believe in. Scripture and friendship. A Simple Rhythm, a fierce song. Good news, an Ordinary Hospitality.

Here on this downtown sidewalk, people stomping by, stumbling by, walking out of bars, walking out of grocery stores, napping on benches. People are a great heaving furnace to me, their own mighty ocean coming my way. People, any people really, are always too much, a relentless churning admixture of wounded, selfish, bullied, and troubled. All those things trading foreground and background and yet somehow all working together to make other people feel like much too much. People don't resolve. The blend of those things remains in the best they do and the best we do. That blend of things as they talk, as they walk on by, as they leave grocery stores and bars.

All our pride and lies, our troubles and losses churning, churning. All the trouble we're in, all the losses we've had, all the lies we've been told. And pride our only shepherd. And all those things churning, churning, churning in someone. All the things coming toward them, all the things going on inside them. The mixture of all those things going on. You can see it in their faces. You can see they're about to start flailing. You can see they can't cope. You see what they'll do to be okay.

And you try to give them regard. This regard, this sign of the cross, this share in His joy, this anguish and light. This place we meet.

I think of the excruciating stillness required to be with them in this place. To be quiet, simple, and gentle in this place.

To give only regard. A fierce song to sit at the bitter feast of others.

EVERYTHING COMING TOWARD THEM, everything going on inside them. I cannot change that. I cannot change them. All they've lost, all the trouble they're in, all the lies they've been told. I can only give those things that cast His light. I can only be a sign of His company. I can only briefly stand in the furnace with them.

Our trust cannot be in what happens, because we never know what will happen, or what furnace we're in. Our trust can only be in what we offer. The trust He rescues, the attention He leads, the intentions He gives back to us. The intention to be given in His name. This offering, this gift of regard, is holy unto itself, its own sign of the joyful return, its own arrival, its own word about this Word of cleansing, provision, and rest.

This offering, this gift of regard, more real than any outcome. More real than what could happen. I limp on down to psych wards, care homes, and downtown sidewalks with my thinning hair and my big, relaxed clothes. Thinking of the things we must let go of to offer ourselves to the world as it is and to people as they are. Thinking of the crucifixion of certainty. Thinking of what gentleness costs us. Thinking of the gentleness close at hand, what's left when the worst happens and nothing makes sense and everything falls apart.

Limping on down to care homes, psych wards, and downtown sidewalks. And you never know what's gonna set them off or when everything is gonna fall apart and what they'll do to be okay. The kind of furnace you'll be in, the kind of flailing you're in for.

And I see, in all of them, flashes of my pastor. The look he gave when he turned on me and introduced me to some of the worst that happens. I see the wounded honor of a ruined god. The sudden terror of the frightened child. The unconquerable loathing of the complete stranger. A stranger to himself, a god toward me. I see, I feel, the sudden screeching, panicked hostility. I see folks who will drown me.

The hardest thing is having to confront that same look on other people's faces. The look on my pastor's face. That's the look that freaks me out, that I've been running from. To meet that same look on other people's faces and to confront it with the gift of regard.

But the slow pace of this ministry is the privilege of briefly standing in the furnace with them. When I'm around some people I feel all the things I don't want to feel. I love them, but if I'm with them I feel confused and bad.

Because with my pastor's look on their face there soon comes all that flailing, horror, what they'll do to be okay. Spitting on you, screaming at you. Threatening you, clinging to you.

Not because you've done anything, but simply because you're there.

Their faces make me feel like I'm back in that office, back in that place. Their faces make me feel that the worst will happen, that nothing makes sense, that everything will fall apart. The waves so big. The serpent so close. Crumbly, flickering, helpless. And the only thing that counts as me, the only thing that feels like me, is the willingness to feel that way. The willingness to give regard to them and to myself. An odder, kinder, gentler light. The willingness to give regard. To go do this and share in Christ together.

It's a willingness Christ wins for me each day. Cleansed and presented by this good news. Presented as this offering. All through His Spirit. And all of it a mending.

But what do I have for the ruined god, the frightened child, and the complete stranger except the gift of regard? What is there to do except confront them, moment by moment, with the means of grace and the gift of regard? To stare them down with good news, and a more Ordinary Hospitality? To keep a Simple Rhythm and learn a fierce song?

They will give you their rudeness, refusal, hostility, and contempt. They will be terrifyingly selfish. You will give them regard. You have chosen stillness instead of flailing. Regard instead of vengeance. This good news and a more Ordinary Hospitality.

But you are the only one playing by those rules, and you will have to forgive them, even while they're still talking to you.

It is often not the spitting or the thrashing that is the hardest. It is the tone they take with you. The way they say it.

The only mercy I have is that now I know that most people cannot help their tone. And people who are hurt, scared, and upset are at the mercy of their bad tone. Too much has happened for them to be gentle—with you, with themselves, with anyone.

It's scary to think that such dark and mysterious things drive our most basic behavior. Instincts, hidden algorithms of mind and body. Things we can't get a good look at, things lurking behind us, and when we turn and look over our shoulder they're gone. My one consolation—for myself, for everyone—is that most of those things seem to be about what we'll do to be okay. The key to regard, to this sign of forgiveness, is to understand that folks are at the mercy of the tremendous things inside themselves. They are unable, at least initially, to not be hostile. Regard waits and wades through that initial hostility.

What is regard if not this place where we forgive people in real time for what they're like and what they're doing? Forgiving them in real time with our thinning hair, our big, relaxed clothes. Limping toward care homes, psych wards, and downtown sidewalks with good news and a Crucified Heart.

With only regard, only the gentleness close at hand, we let go of the precious thing called outcomes. Believing that this offer, this regard, is more real than any outcome. It casts its own light. It is its own sign of that brighter light, that deeper note of rest. We commit ourselves to the gentleness close at hand, to a radiance that speaks of Christ, to our most basic, tender, and visible sign that there is good news and that this news is true. So that offerings can be offerings, so that offerings can be revelation.

We let go of the silent assumption that we are only willing to be with people we can fix. We slowly let go of things working out and people getting better so that we can simply announce instead. Our hope is in His dying and rising and the few precious signs that this news is true. Those few good things that are not lies.

Limping toward care homes, psych wards, and downtown sidewalks. Heading toward difficult people, heading toward sad spaces, with the tender, stubborn light of regard. The sign of His cross. This anguish and light. This place we meet. This table at the end of the world.

"I HEARD YOU TALK TO THE PEOPLE no one wants," said the barista at the coffee shop, before I limped on down to see them. I think on that. I think of what five years of limping on down to care homes and psych wards has turned me into.

Not the successful pastor of a thriving church. Not even the thriving pastor of an unsuccessful church. Not even a pastor at all.

Not a pastor, and not a social worker. A guy who goes out there and talks to people no one wants to talk to, for the deep gladness of just being there. To give regard, and be given in His name, and given to His joy.

I work with an organization, a sponsoring parish. I'm out there, but not just out there. There was a commissioning service. I knelt down in front of other pastors and elders with my thinning hair and my big, relaxed clothes. In my big floppy flannel. I took vows. I was appointed to the office of evangelist. Part-time evangelist, kinda sorta chaplain.

In this service, these words were said by other people who were there:

> Almighty God, whose Son Jesus Christ came to cast fire upon the earth; grant that by the prayers and witnesses of your faithful people a fire of burning zeal may be kindled and pass from heart to heart, and that the Light of Your Son may shine forth bright and clear, and many be brought into the realm of His saving love, through Jesus Christ our Lord. Amen.

These were the words said over me, a part-time chaplain:

> Go forth into the world in peace, be of good courage, hold fast to that which is good, render to no one evil for evil, strengthen the fainthearted and support the weak, help the afflicted, honor all people, love and serve the Lord rejoicing in the power of the Holy Spirit. And the blessing of God Almighty, the Father, the Son, and the Holy Spirit, be upon you and remain with you forever. Amen.

Perhaps the hardest vow I took: to "render to no one evil for evil." To not retaliate, to not even commit the violence of a harsh word or harsh tone. To be gentle in a world not used to gentleness. To not practice the same disregard.

At the service a friend played a song while my wife held my hand, and while my mom and dad sat in the back of the church.

> Jesus, I my cross have taken,
> All to leave and follow Thee.

Destitute, despised, forsaken,
Thou from hence my all shall be.
Perish every fond ambition,
All I've sought or hoped or known.
Yet how rich is my condition!
God and heaven are still my own.

Go, then, earthly fame and treasure,
Come disaster, scorn and pain;
In Thy service, pain is pleasure,
With Thy favor, loss is gain.
I have called Thee Abba Father,
I have stayed my heart on Thee
Storms may howl, and clouds may gather;
All must work for good to me.

Soul, then know thy full salvation
Rise o'er sin and fear and care;
Joy to find in every station,
Something still to do or bear.
Think what Spirit dwells within thee,
Think what Father's smiles are thine,
Think that Jesus died to win thee,
Child of heaven, canst thou repine.

Haste thee on from grace to glory,
Armed by faith, and winged by prayer.
Heaven's eternal days before thee,
God's own hand shall guide us there.

Soon shall close thy earthly mission,
Soon shall pass thy pilgrim days,
Hope shall change to glad fruition,
Faith to sight, and prayer to praise.

SINCE THAT SERVICE I'VE HAD A SEQUEL to that vision of a friend of mine at the table. In the vision I walk up to that table with the odder, kinder, gentler light. I take a piece of bread and a small glass of the wine and step back into darkness with it. The darkness swallows me, and I feel fault lines under my feet. And yet this bread and wine are a little bit of light. Taking the most basic, tender, and visible sign of this good news out into the dark. In that vision, the bread and wine become a light in my hand, a light I hold out.

A dark, an abyss, a looming, ominous, inevitable thing that I hold out the light to, to see if it will still swallow me, still crush me, still pull me.

When I hold the light out, the light is just my face turned toward them, my regard.

In the vision I am a thin man carrying nothing, without all my excess, without everything I thought I should be, without everything I thought I was supposed to be doing, without everything I thought life was supposed to be about, so that I could make my way out, until I achieve singleness of purpose, singleness of heart, until I am just reaching out, holding that flame out, waiting for the darkness to come and take it, but also waiting to see how far it can be taken.

The further you go, the fiercer the song, the gentler the light.

The light of Christ is the regard, the gentleness close at hand, my willingness to look people in the eye. To turn my face to the ruined god, the frightened child, the complete stranger by His gospel and through His Spirit. To gently confront them with the gentleness close at hand, with a more Ordinary Hospitality.

With that vision I hear these words in my father's voice. My father who taught me to be gentle. Who taught me the fierce song. His small talk, his absent-minded tenderness, his cherished decency. His goodness to us. Soaring over his broken hips to reconcile with us.

Words he never said but that I hear in his voice anyway, words that have been my only map out:

> Be gentle, consistent, and never turn your face away.

Don't be afraid of what you find out there. Be gentle, consistent, and never turn your face away. And put your trust only in what He offers, never in what happens.

Go out, grieve better, give regard, be glad. Go out there, with that great serpent, with those great big waves, with that great undertow, feeling so crumbly, flickering, and helpless. Go out there by the power of Word and Spirit, go out there with good news and a simple life, go out there until you find a clearing, until you find out you are the clearing. That your regard is the sign of the cross. Your regard is the anguish and light. Your regard is the table at the end of the world. Your regard is the place we meet. The light that won't go out.

WHAT DOES REGARD DO? It bestows honor. It clothes shame. It rescues trust. It upholds. It reveals. Better, it bears witness to the One who does these things. The gift of regard, the gentleness close at hand. The most basic, tender, and visible sign of the reality of Christ, the forgiveness of sins, the homecoming offered only in Him. It wastes time, it gets nothing done. It is only a sign that Christ has, that Christ will. Only a sign that this news is true.

It is hard to see my gaze not being used for what it's for. To find myself not able to regard people, too busy or too rushed or too pressured. To not be able to be with people.

When would my attention hallow and not devour? When would my attention anoint and not take? When would it uphold and not degrade?

When I was younger, I felt the cringe of my own gaze, the devouring specter of the male gaze. I understood that a lingering glance was not right. I saw that it was not what this was all about. It was not what regard is for.

Regard was supposed to honor rather than devour.

Our gaze was meant to uphold, to hallow, to transfigure one another. Regard was meant to be a goodness. A sign of the only kind of life that ever struck that deeper note of rest. We must grieve the loss of what our regard was meant to do. Our regard was supposed to honor and not devour. It was supposed to uphold and not destroy.

Our gaze was meant for us to uphold, to hallow, to transfigure one another. It was meant for us to use at His table, to see and be seen, to enjoy and be enjoyed.

I struggle for that gaze, that intention. My attention is always elsewhere. My attention is still a wild animal, my eyes still looking for something else, something new, shiny, distracting.

My attention, my gaze, feels like that wild animal. I find myself always looking around. A gaze that never rests. I struggle for a gaze that upholds, a gaze that hallows. A gaze that offers some sign of that brighter light, that darker shade of blue, that deeper note of rest. A gaze that says we are committed to their good. A gaze that says there is nothing but who we are at His table.

The fight has been for my attention, this wild animal, to be a precious coin laid down on the counter of the moment at hand. The struggle has been for more Ordinary Hospitality. To find a table at the end of world.

What we notice is what we notice, but what we look at, what we've decided to look at, is what we've decided this is all about. A gaze won for me by Christ, by a simple life with this good news. Good news that crucifies the heart and prepares us for a more Ordinary Hospitality.

Gently washed back toward the gaze, toward what I most want, toward a simple life with this good news, news that wants to rescue our trust in Him and shepherd our attention toward Him and give us to each other in His name. Cleansed by Word and Spirit and presented at the bitter feast of others.

Giving this regard. Learning His gentleness.

My friend, the handsome, long-haired Mister Rogers, looks at me. I've limped on down to see him but I'm not really there.

"John," he says. "John."

"I'm talking to you," he says. "I'm talking to you."

Our gaze is a gift that clothes shame, that clothes hurt, but how long can we stand it? How long can I stand this fierce song, this obstinate grace? This regard, this grief? That cleanses my hardened heart even as it reveals it?

I hear the edge in my friend's tone. That irritation. And I hear the irritation gathering in my own voice. How can I stand this furnace, this gentleness close at hand? How long can we stare the world down with His forgiveness? How long can I grieve the loss of honor and respect?

How to not reply with snark, sass? How to just say, "I can't just listen to you right now. I can't be there for you right now. Not right now. I have to go. I'm sorry. I'm sorry. Another time. Another time." How to say "No" gently?

How to do all this, when there's only refusal or anguish? When there's only defiance or anguish that seeks the face of Christ? When the only thing that works is regard, and regard is an agony—the agony of love? An agony that seeks the face of Christ through a more Ordinary Hospitality. Given in His name, given to His joy. And what will it be? Revelation or refusal? Our gaze sits at that razor's edge, the beautiful and the intolerable. Regard, the table we set for the bitter feast of others. How long can we sit there? How long can we do this and share in Christ together?

How long could I stand mistreatment? How long can I stand with this loss? How long can I stand to grieve? How long can I stand this gentleness and grief pointed toward gladness?

I ask. I wonder. This regard is such grief, such a furnace still. To stand there without certainty. To stand there when you're hurt, scared, and upset, and to give regard. I love my friend, but he makes no sense. I never understand what he's saying and so I try to not stick around.

But I stay there and nod even though I'm miserable, even though I don't understand. I stand there by the coffee and nod. Nodding and acknowledging only that whatever he's telling me is important or he wouldn't be saying it. I'm in this furnace, caught in this regard and its grief. I'm busy, I'm important, this is worthless, pointless, stupid, futile. I don't have time for this. It is anguish to me, to the little boy I still am who can't stand things.

Anguish or refusal? Anguish or defiance? Is it true that anguish is still the color blue? That anguish still strikes that deeper note of rest? That this longing, toil, and striving is still our share in who He is and what He's done? That anguish still speaks of Christ?

That this anguish works with Christ? That this anguish is Christ working with us? That it matters very little who they are, and matters very much whose they are? That it matters very little who we serve, and very much Who our serving announces? And the fellowship He's building? And that we work with Him in the building of His fellowship?

"John? John, are you listening?"

And yet standing here in this furnace of wasted time, this life blurs with the world to come. My friend laughs and smiles. I see him. I see who he is: honored guest and humble servant of this table. This is someone I'll enjoy forever at that table, and this is the joyful work of seeing him now. The anguish and light of seeing him now. So that anguish is a song as well.

People can be changed, but only by the revelation of Christ to the wounded soul and the hardened heart. We can all be changed, but only by this good news, and those few small signs that this news is true.

Lord, is it Your grief we enter? Your grief, when You bore the unacceptable, the intolerable, Your face turned to us still? Is regard our share in who You are and what You've done? Is regard our participation in Your grief? Can we learn Your gentleness? Can we enter Your grief? How, Lord? How? By what mysteries do we bear such things? Is it true You have accounted for all losses?

I BELIEVE IN REGARD, and I believe in what regard becomes. I believe regard becomes company, as dying becomes rising, as gentleness becomes grief. As good news become the attempt of prayer. I believe company is the vindication of regard. That the people we look at become the people we walk with.

Life is too much. Our suffering is too much. Only the broken body of our Savior can hold those losses—especially the loss of security. The loss of security and assurance is a loss held in a crucified body that rose again, and we are a sign of it as we keep people company. The sign of what only that feast can do.

We keep people company only as a kind of witness, only as a sign of the Christ who is the companion. Our companionship is a kind of grief. We grieve the loss of outcomes, we grieve the loss of what we thought would happen, we grieve the fact that people, places, and things often don't get better, on this long, slow walk we take together, out of pride and lies, through trouble and loss, toward meaning and rest.

You sit there as they sit there, you eat as they eat, you wait with them as they wait, at their doctor's appointments, their meetings with social workers, their court hearings, at their family reunions they don't know if they can't stand to go to. It's their journey they're on, it's their return to the feast. All you can do is keep witness and be a sign of Him. A sign that nothing that happens changes what this is all about. The Person this is all about.

Company is kept, but nothing is fixed, nothing is better. We give those things up to offer something better: the sign that this news is true. A vigil is kept. Company is a kind of witness, a basic, tender, and visible sign that it is only Christ who walks us through trouble and loss and the fear of all we'll lose and all the trouble we're in. And to only do this, to only be responsible for what we offer, is grief. The company we keep: our entrance into His grief.

You have to be prepared for it to not matter that you're there—except that it matters that you're there. And for it to only be a sign that this news is true.

You keep company with the ruined god, the frightened child, the complete stranger. You withstand their wounded honor, their sudden terror, and their unconquerable loathing. You withstand it by Word and Spirit, by the means of grace. You accompany their moods, make your way with them in that ocean, keep them company in this place where the worst happens and nothing makes sense and everything falls apart.

People need company, and they need company in particular across thresholds, in transitions, those spaces between what was and what will be. That is where company is needed. That is where company is kept: through trouble and loss. Even the loss of bad things is loss.

The wounded honor, the sudden terror, the unconquerable loathing, is heightened in the in-betweenness of things. As they make their way through what life's like, as they live in that ocean, company is needed in the in-betweenness of things, where nothing is clear, whether nothing is known for sure, where we don't know where we'll land or if we'll land. Company is a gift to folks in the in-betweenness of things. It doesn't mean anything other than that Christ is risen and you are with them and you are going to be around.

Only a sign that this news is true. That nothing that happens changes what life's about. Our regard and company: this way to be together, this anguish and light, this place. Our regard and our company: the table at the end of the world.

Good company means we trade routines for heroics, and we choose rhythms over grand acts. A simple coffee each week means more, does more, than a heroic plunge every now and then. It announces better news. A ride to appointments means more than a big donation. A phone call every other day means more than bailing someone out when they're drunk. It means having less to give and giving it as well as we can. It means we can give something much better than solutions. We can give our most basic, visible, and tender sign this news is true. When we're only responsible for what we offer, we work with Christ, and we offer only those things by which Christ gathers a people to Himself.

Being good company means watching people suffer. It means watching people fall apart. It means being with people who won't get better. Our company can never be conditioned on them getting better. We must leave room for people to not get better. We must accept that we are only a sign that this news is true. Only a sign of the table in this place. We only announce the One who has accounted for every loss, who turns our loss to sorrow, our sorrow to longing, and our longing to joy.

And we only do it for the goodness of the thing itself and for the sake of the table we serve. We offer a gentleness that points us toward grief and gladness.

And so we find that company isn't about needs—although it is. It is about thresholds, transition. It's about crossing over. From what life's like to what life's about. Walking with folks from what was to what will be, walking with them past every premonition of disaster. From what life's like to what life's about. You go with them into whatever room they're stuck in. You hold out the light of regard. You walk with them until they find a clearing or until things really do fall apart. And you do it for the goodness of the thing itself, for the Person it speaks of.

AND IT WILL BE HARD, because they will ask of you more than you can give. That is the grief of good company. The grief is what you can't be for other people. Grieving what you can't offer people so that you can give them what you actually can. And the grief is how little it seems to mean.

People are hurt, scared, and upset. They don't know what they're doing. And everything is falling apart and everyone is flailing.

They don't understand that they pull on you too hard with what they need, push on you too hard with what they want. Wanting to take things back and make things right, playing by those rules and not even knowing it. Ruined gods, terrified children, complete strangers, and not even knowing it. You can see it on their faces. You can see it so clearly. But it is not clear to them. They are even blind to their own flailing. They are even blind to their own hostility. They are even blind to the true horror of what they'll do be okay. And you learn to be gentle with those who cannot be gentle with you. Too much has happened for them to be any other way.

When you give regard, company, you give a limit—a boundary. You admit you are not a savior, just a servant. You are not good news. You are just a sign that this news is true. Your regard tells them "No" even as it tells them "Yes." Giving what you can, you renounce what is not yours to give.

And so you give what you can. You give it even though it doesn't seem to mean much. You give it even though it doesn't seem to matter. And yet, and yet, without good company people won't make it. They won't make it over, they won't make it through, on this long, slow walk we take together.

6

THE LOOK OF THOSE TRANSFIGURED

"For the sake of the house of the LORD our God,
I will seek your good."
—Psalm 122:9

I believe in the Look of Those Transfigured. One of those few good things that are not lies.

I still don't believe in things working out. But I believe in the regard we give and the company we keep. These few small signs that this news is true. And I believe that, by the power of Word and Spirit, the regard we give and the company we keep become places for people to be. The people we look at and walk with end up at the things we do. These places where they will not be devoured or destroyed. These places where they can be changed by signs of Sabbath rest, signs this news is true. Our deepest longing—to see them changed, by this good news and the few small signs that this news is true.

We make third spaces. We make stoops. We make places for people to be.

How did it happen? How do the regard we give and the company we keep become places for people to be? I don't know.

Perhaps it's just an intuition: When you give regard and come alongside, you start to look for a place of rest. A place to sit. Some kind of stoop.

Abused in an office. Mended in coffee shops and a sad, green truck. Limping on down to care homes, psych wards, and downtown sidewalks. Arriving on stoops.

What are these third spaces? These stoops? They are our word about a Word, this Word of cleansing, provision, and rest. They are a sign of the joyful end, the end of pride, lies, trouble, and loss, chaos and disaster. The end of all we've lost, all the trouble we're in, all the lies we've been told, and the pride that's been our only shepherd.

These third spaces, these stoops, are my joy, but they are the hardest thing I do. I have no mind, it seems, for events. I am overwhelmed, tossed back and forth in a churning ocean of other logistics and other people's moods. Every space we make seems to be choked and surrounded with premonitions and harassments. This ocean. This place of pride and lies, trouble and loss, chaos and disaster.

There are times when it feels like we should all go home. That we are all too hurt, scared, and upset to be here, too hurt, scared, and upset to share a table or sit on a stoop. That spaces like this can't hold together if they're full of ruined gods, frightened children, and complete strangers.

I sit around with other people, people we've listened to and walked with. And we're all on a stoop, except that the stoop is our weekly craft table. And they are getting mad at each other. Tension is rising. Unbearable tension. It feels like the center will not hold. Everything will fall apart. These places are so fragile, and yet they are our peace, our most basic, tender, and visible sign of the reality of Christ, the forgiveness of sins, and the homecoming offered only in Him. Our sign of the only kind of life that has ever had that deeper note of rest.

The regard we've given, the company we've kept, means we look for stoops, we create these spaces of rest and just sit there and see if the center will hold. We arrive at stoops. We arrive at our big dumb try. Abused in an office. Mended in coffee shops. Limping on down to care homes, psych wards, downtown sidewalks. Arriving on these stoops.

Making stoops. To see if there is such a thing as a place we're all supposed to be. To see if we can make a place like that out of the gentleness close at hand.

To make it out of craft supplies and the gentleness close at hand. That was all we had initially. Some empty spaces, some leftover craft supplies, and the gentleness close at hand.

Here at the weekly craft table, voices get high, tensions rise. Chairs scuffle. This anguish and light. This place we meet. Nothing yet, but maybe soon. I scribble on a sheet of paper: *Unbearable tension, unbearable love, unbearable tension, unbearable love, unbearable tension, unbearable love.*

And I think to myself, *sacred and unacceptable.* The inevitability of good news, the inevitability of any sign of this good news: other people. Sacred and unacceptable. Sacred and unacceptable.

On Fridays our church sanctuary becomes a coffeehouse for the community. The centerpiece of that coffeehouse is a giant craft table—another big dumb try. We shove six tables together, sometimes eight or ten or even twelve. We throw tablecloths with bold prints over the tables so it looks like one big table in the center of the room. We set out gel pens, paintbrushes, canvases, coloring books, birdhouses, and chunks of wood. It is a craft buffet. This craft table, this anguish and light. This place we meet.

The stained-glass window of wasted time. The light drops in from the stained-glass window to illuminate a giant table strewn with things we found at Michael's.

My friend is there, one leg draped over the other. My friend, a younger looking, long-haired Mister Rogers. My friend, a thin man in his late forties with a gentle smile, a sense of humor, and acute schizophrenia.

Elbows on the table. His hand up, two fingers the air like he's holding a cigarette no one can see. Or like he's about to introduce a topic for discussion, except he never does. He won't do art but he'll sit at the table and preside. He is loved here, and I think he knows that. He doesn't have to say much—I think he knows that too. And I think in that moment, his hand in the air, he knows: nothing left but to share in who He is and what He's done, nothing left but who we are at the table.

The look of those upheld. The look of an honored guest. The Look of Those Transfigured.

I sit and listen while I color something. There is music in the background. We do singer-songwriter, outlaw country, folk. Sad, folksy, melodic. The music means people don't feel like they have to talk. They can just listen. The crafts make people feel like they don't have to talk. They can just do something with their hands. People can just be there. This other way to be together. This place they're supposed to be. We think they know that.

The craft table is also strewn with coffee and donuts. People eat and work and sit and talk and the goodness of it is the goodness of the thing itself. This way to be together. The time we share. The joy we offer, the joy in offering. Even when it's just wasted time.

These folks have been hurt. A lot has happened. Ordinary conversation is often too painful, too hard. They cannot handle direct face-to-face questions. It's too much, too intense. They need a gentler way to be completely involved. Gel pens. Uno. A gentler way to be together. A gentler way to let everyone know this news is true.

Sometimes no one is there, but often enough it's full. This bright light, this darker shade of blue, this deeper note of rest.

I step back sometimes and look at it. People who have no reason to be talking are talking. There is an ease. We can be quiet, simple, and gentle in this place. An old tough guy draws a portrait and we tell him it's great. A shy woman eventually tries the gel pens and sits there for hours.

We've done this every week for four years, offering this big dumb thing again and again. Learning to offer it, learning what it means to offer this and nothing else for a while. To only offer regard, company, and a place of rest. To only be a sign this news is true. To offer it to people who may not get better. To offer it anyway. To give regard, and be given in His name and given to

His joy. To see Him more clearly as we offer a more Ordinary Hospitality.

For a while the table is more real than what is wrong and what can happen. Sometimes I simply can't believe it:

Other people are the chaos and other people are the shore. It's other people who are sacred and other people who are unacceptable. It's other people I can't stand and other people I love. A table at the end of the world. A Table Called Mercy. The table in this place.

Abused in an office. Mended in coffee shops and a sad, green truck. Limping on down to psych wards, care homes, and downtown sidewalks. Arriving on these stoops. Cleansed by this news, presented on these stoops. And all through His Spirit and all of it a mending.

THERE IS ANOTHER THING WE TRY. The people who come to the craft table come to the church basement once a month for a thing called Evensong and Open Mic. We push back old junk and chairs and clear a space for donuts and light. There is a table for donuts, pizza, and coffee. Good donuts, good pizza, bad coffee. Strewn around the place, on a stage made of old wooden pallets and around an electric organ, there are lights. Big lights, small lights, Christmas lights, outdoor lights. We put the lights on. Those lights that speak of this Light. There are lights hanging everywhere, braided around the idea of Light.

I've taken my illuminated tiles of Scriptures and glued them onto lamp shades to make a thing called a lamp of God. There are ten of those lamps around the basement, on pianos and sitting in odd corners. I've made junk sing.

People come in early and sit. They are our friends, people who would otherwise be wandering around. I put on music. Folksy stuff, bluesy stuff. Banjo stuff. The whole thing is like a speakeasy. The whole thing is darkness, beauty, and light. That brighter light, that darker shade of blue, that deeper note of rest.

The people trickle in. I invite a lot of folks but it is the people we see around downtown who come. A few of the crushed. Some of the people the worst has happened to.

They come and I pass out our worship bulletins. Bulletins made out of things from those ugly books. An Evensong frankensteined together from old liturgies, old hymns, and Gregorian chants. I've picked the most beautiful things I can. Sung confessions, sung Scriptures, sung prayers. I find the most beautiful music I can still play, the most beautiful music made of only quarter notes. Little notes to make a song. I've made it a call and response. I sing a line and they sing a line. I sing a line and I wait to see if they will sing a line back to me.

I'm sitting on a makeshift stage. I'm sitting on a stoop. I'm holding an accordion as I sing and play. A friend is on the keys. I'm up there, lights coiled round me, with my thinning hair, my big, relaxed clothes. With a fanny pack and an accordion.

Part-time evangelist, kinda sorta chaplain. I don't really sing usually. My voice is no good. But I'm singing. I'm holding an accordion I can't play and singing to them even though I can't sing.

I feel the humiliation. This big dumb try. This serpent coiled close, this almost certain disaster. I'm showing a bunch of crushed people Gregorian chants, not knowing if they think this is stupid, not knowing if they will join in. Not knowing if they will keep singing. Not knowing if they even care.

I'm out on a limb with an accordion, my thinning hair, my big, relaxed clothes. I'm out on a limb and I'm singing and I'm waiting to fall. In the ocean, at the table. Presented at the bitter feast of others.

It's other people. I'm singing to other people. I'm waiting to see if I can be with other people, and take a seat at the bitter feast of others.

What is this? My song about His table. My big dumb try.

What is happening? I am being given. A special kind of being given.

Learning to serve His table. Learning that only joy will do.

What is this? All my gentleness, all my grief, all my gladness. My brightest light, my darkest shade of blue. And my deep note of rest.

Given in His name. Given to His joy. Cleansed and presented. All at once, and day after day. And now. Right now.

"Into your hands, O Lord, I commend my spirit," I sing.

"For you have redeemed me, O God of truth," they answer.

NOTES

Pages 148, 156	Jesus's words from John 14:19.
Page 180	"New Wine," by Brooke Ligertwood, produced by Michael Guy Chislett, Hillsong Music, 2018.
Page 210, 218	"With your constant love you led," *The Book of Common Prayer (2019)* (Anglican Liturgy Press, 2019), 83; based on words from Exodus 15:13.
Page 221	Psalm 118:17.
Page 282–84	"Jesus, I My Cross Have Taken," Henry Francis Lyte, 1825.
Page 297	Psalm 122:9.